ROSES

'*Love*' (Grandiflora Rose)

By the Editors of Sunset Books and Sunset Magazine

Lane Publishing Co.• Menlo Park, California

Friends of the Rose...

Since the beginnings of recorded history, people have been writing about roses. It is, therefore, no small undertaking to distill so many centuries of rose lore into one book. Take almost any aspect of the rose—history, culture, the roses themselves—and an entire volume could be devoted to it. Fortunately, experienced rosarians not only are knowledgeable but also have been very generous with their time in helping us select and evaluate basic information to benefit the novice rose grower and tomorrow's dyed-in-the-wool rose enthusiast.

This book presents a summation of this accumulated knowledge for today's gardening public, and we are grateful to many contemporary rose friends who are guardians of centuries of rose wisdom. For their invaluable aid which led to the material you find in the following pages we wish to acknowledge the valuable assistance of Dr. R. C. Allen, Tucson, Arizona; David H. Berg, Bloomfield, Connecticut; the late Edwin A. Birge, Carrollton, Georgia; Charles P. Dawson, Simpsonville, Kentucky; Fred Edmunds, Wilsonville, Oregon; George Haight, San Jose, California; Don Herzog, Sebastopol, California; Mrs. Muriel Humenick, Diamond Springs, California; Rudy Kalmbach, Portland, Oregon; Joseph Klima, Kentfield, California; Frank J. Lacoma, Omaha, Nebraska; Ross V. Lahr, Littleton, Colorado; John C. MacGregor IV, San Marino, California; Dr. C. A. Rohrer, Winona, Minnesota; the late Carson Scoggins, Shreveport, Louisiana; the late Dorothy Stemler, Watsonville, California; John van Barneveld, La Habra, California; Howard Walters, Houston, Texas; Miriam Wilkins, El Cerrito, California; and Barbara Worl, Menlo Park, California.

Edited by Philip Edinger

Design
Timothy Bachman

Illustrations
Vernon Koski

COVER: 'Double Delight'
From the moment it was first evaluated in the All-America Rose Selection trials, this distinctive hybrid tea has consistently earned high marks for both performance and beauty. Specific information on it appears on page 47. Photographed by Ells Marugg.

Sunset Books
    Editor, David E. Clark
    Managing Editor, Elizabeth L. Hogan

Sixth printing May 1987
(Updated 1986)

CONTENTS

Special Features

Introducing the Queen

When you invite the rose to grace your garden, you welcome not only a plant that provides great beauty but also one that proudly carries a rich heritage of legend and history. Inhabitant of Eden, perfumed blossom of ancient Babylonian and Persian gardens, sacred flower of Aphrodite and Venus, the rose has been a special flower to all cultures that have known it.

Just one look at the modern rose will illustrate why it has been repeatedly called the "queen of flowers." Yet it was the Greek poetess Sappho who bestowed this title on the rose—in 600 B.C., when roses were far removed from their modern refinement. Obviously there was "something" even then about the simple rose that caused it to stand out from other flowers in a regal and femininely beautiful way. Roses did not escape the notice of another literary Greek; Homer referred to them in both his epics, the *Odyssey* and the *Iliad.* And in a strictly formal reference, the natural scientist Theophrastus wrote a botanical account of roses in the 4th century B.C.

Although the Greeks may have been the first to give it a title, earlier civilizations held the rose in equally high regard but chose to demonstrate their affection through other art forms. Asian coins minted 4,000 years ago are adorned with the rose motif. Frescoes dating from 1,600 B.C. uncovered on the Mediterranean island of Crete distinctly portray

blossoms of single roses. Of similar antiquity are rose-inspired architectural decorations found in ruins of the Assyrian and Babylonian civilizations that once flourished in present-day Iraq.

While all these ancient cultures glorified and stylized the rose, it remained for the Romans to bring it down to earth: they loved roses in a very physical sense. Hardly a public or private ceremony took place without roses playing a part. Blossoms were used at weddings, funerals, and military ceremonies; they were important as party decorations (for the room *and* the guests), in perfumery, and for medicinal purposes. A wealthy Roman could be bathed in rose water, drink rose wine, eat confections made from roses, and party in rooms strewn with their petals. Because of such widespread use, commercial rose growing became a profitable Roman industry.

The decorative use of roses reached a frenzy during post-Christian Roman times. Rose petals at one festive gathering, for example, were so deep that a number of the guests suffocated in them—helped along, probably, by too much rose wine. On the scholarly side, Pliny, in his *Natural History,* recorded valuable information concerning the identification of the different types, colors, and growth habits of the roses then in cultivation.

FROM ROMAN TIMES TO THE 20TH CENTURY

Since they were identified so closely with Roman excesses, it's no wonder that roses fell out of favor with the early Christian church. Fortunately, this stigma was cast aside rather quickly, and the rose became the symbol, instead, for survivors of religious persecution. In addition, the white rose often symbolized the Immaculate Conception of the Virgin Mary. In fact, the term for a garden of roses—"rosary"—was applied to the series of prayers related to the life of Christ and the Virgin Mary. Of all its religious expressions, however, probably the most magnificent is the "rose window," a standard component of medieval cathedrals.

From the earliest days of chivalry, the rose was a favored motif for heraldic crests and a design element in the banners and shields of numerous European noblemen. Several English monarchs—beginning with Edward I in 1272—adopted the rose as their badge. Roses were made tragically famous in the conflict between the English houses of York and Lancaster, whose emblems were, respectively, a white and a red rose. The culmination of this conflict was known, of course, as the War of the Roses.

During the thousand or so years between the fall of the western Roman empire and the Renaissance, interest in roses in western Europe was kept alive largely in the hundreds of Christian monasteries scattered throughout the continent. Not only were roses important symbolically to the religion, but also they had a number of medicinal uses ascribed to them.

Although Romans cultivated a number of different roses from among those growing in their empire, and later Christians perpetuated these sorts in cloistered gardens, credit for widespread dissemination of many rose species and natural hybrids must go to the Moslem Arabs. Not long after the fall of Rome, they began extending their holdings from the Near East into western Europe on one hand and into the Far East on the other. In Persia, India, and China, they encountered entirely different roses which they carried westward, just as they took western species to the East. Many of these roses persist even today in lands around the Mediterranean and in the Near East. Some of them, however, went unnoticed by early European botanists and did not enter into the mainstream of rose development until "rediscovered" during the 17th and 18th centuries by Europeans venturing into Asia.

An imperial patroness

From the viewpoint of modern rose culture, nothing is historically so important as the enthusiasm for roses generated by the Empress Josephine, wife of France's Napoleon I. At her disposal she had extensive resources and influence, enabling her to collect and maintain nearly all species and hybrids known at that time. Begun in 1804, the rose collection at the imperial château Malmaison reached its zenith ten years later—with about 250 different roses represented. The fame of Josephine's rose garden was international, and so great was respect for it that the British—then at war with France—actually permitted plants found on captured French ships to be sent on to Malmaison. At the end of hostilities in 1815, occupying British troops were ordered to protect the garden from harm.

The Empress also summoned a group of artists to her rose garden so that the forms and colors of her collected roses might be preserved for posterity. Among these artists was Pierre-Joseph Redouté—the "Raphael of the flowers"—whose water-color paintings of Josephine's roses later were published in a three-volume work, *Les Roses,* accompanied by botanical descriptions by Claude Antoine Thory. To this day the beauty and detail of Redouté's illustrations remain unsurpassed.

A brief consideration of the most prominent types of roses in Josephine's garden will give an idea of what was grown popularly up to that time and what were the ancestors of our modern roses.

Gallicas. More than half of the Empress Josephine's 250-odd roses were gallicas—varieties, and in some cases hybrids, of *Rosa gallica.* Known also as the French rose, the species grows wild in western Europe, its flowers pink to light red in color. The color range of its hybrids extends from rich maroon and dark red shades through light pink and a number of striped combinations. Typically, the gallicas are very hardy, adaptable, vigorous, richly colored, and fragrant. Flowering only once each year, they were the most popular class of roses until the mid-nineteenth century advent of repeat-flowering roses with blossoms of similar appeal.

Among the gallicas still sold by specialists are *Rosa gallica* 'Officinalis' ("Apothecary Rose"), semi-double crimson red; 'Charles de Mills', very double, varying from lilac through rich red shades to purple; 'Camaieux' (1830), semi-double to double, the blush white petals striped with rose pink and later fading to magenta, purple, and lilac; 'Tuscany Superb', semi-double, blackish maroon, lighted by prominent gold stamens.

Damasks. Josephine had only eight of these somewhat mysterious roses. The mystery surrounds their place of origin and, most importantly, how some of them acquired the ability to flower more than once yearly. What was called *Rosa damascena* made its first documented appearance in the ancient Near East (its name is taken from Damascus, Syria) and seems to have been brought west by Phoenician traders or Greek colonials, if not by the Egyptians. Romans knew the repeat-flowering autumn damask as the "Rose of Paestum" (or of Cyrinae or Carthage), and its likeness appears on frescoes in Pompeii. Many centuries later, Spanish missionaries brought it to North America, where it is known as the "Rose of Castile."

Twentieth-century research has shed some possible light on the origins of damask roses. Both the once-blooming summer damasks and the repeat-flowering autumn damasks are of ancient hybrid origin, presumably involving *Rosa gallica*. The other ancestor of the summer damasks probably is *Rosa phoenicea,* a once-blooming musk rose relative, native to Israel and Syria. The autumn damasks, however, appear to derive from the old autumn-blooming musk rose—closely related to *Rosa phoenicea* but blooming in late summer continuously through fall, until stopped by frost.

The damask fragrance is legendary; even today acres of a summer damask type are grown in Bulgaria to produce the petals from which the fragrance "attar of roses" is extracted. Until the China roses made their European debut late in the 1700s, the autumn damasks were the only roses to repeat bloom.

The ancient autumn damask (*Rosa damascena bifera* or *Rosa bifera*) is still available commercially. It is a tall and open to rangy plant bearing informally double, intensely fragrant pink blossoms. Among the once-flowering summer damask types are *Rosa damascena versicolor* ("York and Lancaster"), light pink or blush white, or a mixture of the two colors; 'Celsiana' (before 1750), semi-double pink fading to nearly white; 'Madame Hardy', very double white, opening flat with the petals carefully arranged around a green "eye" in the flower center; 'Leda' ("Painted Damask"), very double white, the outer petals tipped in rosy red.

Albas. Only nine alba roses grew in Josephine's garden, and of the early forms of *Rosa alba* and its later hybrids only a few are still in cultivation. But those that remain include some of the most valuable old roses for garden use. The original albas were natural hybrids between the damask rose and a white form of the dog rose (*Rosa canina*), the combination sweetening the damask parent's tangy perfume and producing plants of vigorous, upright habit and exceptional disease resistance. All the albas blossom only in spring, in delicate tints of pink or white. Most will tolerate some shade, and their highly adaptable growth habit suits them for use as self-supporting shrubs; or as "climbers," attached to walls or fences; or, more closely pruned, as bedding roses.

Albas available today include 'Maiden's Blush' (before 1400), loosely double light pink; 'Félicité Parmentier' (1836), globular, pink-centered white flowers; 'Königin von Dänemark' (1826), strong carmine-pink fading lighter, highly fragrant, and very double.

Centifolias. About one-eighth of the Malmaison collection consisted of *Rosa centifolia* varieties and hybrids. The centifolia or "cabbage rose," produced by back-crossing a form of *Rosa alba* with its damask parent, had up to 100 petals packed into each flower; the fullness of its blossom was distinctive and unique. Colors of its sports and hybrids included white and all shades of pink, but none of the rich reds found in the gallicas. The centifolias have only one flowering season, but they have two claims to fame. One is their intense, sweet fragrance, still the main source of true rose essence for the French perfume industry. The other is their production of mutations in various sizes, forms, and colors—among them the moss roses (below) and some of the first miniature garden roses.

'Fantin Latour', from the mid-19th century, bears typical centifolia blossoms, pale pink and highly fragrant. 'De Meaux' (17th century) is one of the centifolia miniatures—1-inch flowers in shades of pink, leaves in proportion to flower size, on a bush reaching up to three feet tall. 'Chapeau de Napoleon' (1826), also known as "Crested Moss," bridges the gap between centifolias and the true moss roses: flowers are typical centifolia but the green calyx that covers the bud before it opens is elaborately fringed.

Moss roses. Anomalies of the rose kingdom, these appeared unexpectedly, were beloved for their charming difference, but contributed nothing to the development of other classes. The first moss rose appeared, perhaps around 1700, as a mutation of *Rosa centifolia*. To the charm of a full-petaled flower, the moss roses added a dense covering of balsam-scented glands on the unopened buds, flower stems, and sometimes even leaflets.

Moss rose types also developed by mutation from

(Continued on page 10)

Old European Roses

The flowers on these two pages belong to the classes of old garden roses developed in Europe and the southern Mediterranean lands before 1800. With the exception of autumn damask, they are selections or hybrids of European species and have but one profuse flowering period—in spring. All make fine garden shrubs and are still available for planting in modern gardens.

De Meaux (Centifolia)

Leda (Damask)

Tuscany Superb (Gallica)

Deuil de Paul Fontaine (Moss)

Félicité Parmentier (Alba)

autumn damask and gallica roses, but the difference is obvious to the touch: a centifolia "moss" is soft, while a damask "moss" is distinctly prickly. In Josephine's time, all moss rose varieties were the result of mutation; only in later years were some achieved by hybridization.

"Common moss" or *Rosa centifolia muscosa* is presumed to be the original moss mutation—clear pink flowers crammed with petals and opening flat around a green central "eye." 'Gloire des Mousseux' (1852) is in varying shades of pink; 'Comtesse de Murinais' (1843) is probably a damask moss, blush fading to white with a green central "eye." Repeat-flowering moss roses include 'Deuil de Paul Fontaine' (1873), double blossoms in shades of rose red through purple; 'Madame Louis Lévêque' (1873), light pink and very full petaled; 'Salet' (1854), many petals of clear pink.

Chinas. At the same time that the awareness of roses was being fostered by Josephine, the British, French, and Dutch were making important horticultural discoveries in the Orient—a part of the world largely out of contact with western Europe until the 17th and 18th centuries. The East India Companies of these three countries established posts in China and India where, among many fascinating new plants, there were roses quite different from those familiar in Europe. These were collected and sent back to individuals and botanical gardens in northern Europe, from which they often were distributed as quickly as new plants could be propagated.

The first Oriental roses to reach western Europe arrived in the 18th century. With their introduction into England and France, they attracted the attention of horticulturists. Their popularity was assured because, in contrast to all other known roses, the Chinas came close to being everblooming. Two forms were brought in at about the same time: 'Parson's Pink China' ('Old Blush') and 'Slater's Crimson China', both varieties having been grown in Chinese gardens for centuries. Overwhelmingly in their favor was their frequency of bloom; their liabilities were a tenderness to cold and, compared with damasks and gallicas, their slight fragrance. Because the Malmaison collection attempted to encompass all the roses then known, Josephine collected as many of the Chinas as she could get: about 21.

'Parson's Pink China' is still catalogued—as 'Old Blush', semi-double rose pink flowers almost constantly produced in small clusters. More double, but on a smaller bush, is 'Hermosa' (1840). 'Archduke Charles' (mid-19th century) has double flowers of light and medium pink, the color deepening to nearly red as the blooms age. 'Mutabilis' is a bronze-leaved chameleon: single flowers begin a buff yellow and change to pink and finally red as they age.

Tea roses. Just the mention of their name can evoke memories of "grandmother's garden" or images of gracious ante-bellum Southern estates. These were the truly overblooming pink, cream, buff, and light yellow roses (usually with weak "necks" below the flowers) that were standard components of 19th and early 20th century rose gardens in mild-winter areas. Countless times referred to as the "aristocrats of the rose world," tea roses left their flower form and overall refinement as legacies to modern roses—along with some of their intolerance of cold winter temperatures.

The tea roses are an ancient hybrid amalgam of the China rose and the rampantly climbing *Rosa gigantea*. The first of these, 'Hume's Blush Tea-scented China', reached Europe in 1810 and was one of the treasured new introductions to Josephine's collection. A yellow form, 'Park's Yellow Tea-scented China', was sent from China to England in 1824. ("Tea-scented" described their fragrance: that of a good quality Chinese black tea.) Basically, from these two tea roses was developed a race of elegant, though tender, garden roses whose popularity lasted for about eighty years, until they were superseded by their hardier offspring, the hybrid teas (see page 14).

The importance of tea and China roses can hardly be overestimated. They are the source of the modern rose's capacity for continually repeated bloom, a trait that we take for granted; and the teas were the first roses to feature the long, pointed bud. Tea roses are extremely long-lived plants, and some of them are highly disease resistant.

Tea roses sold today include the soft pink 'Duchesse de Brabant' (1857), the buds shaped like tulips; 'Catherine Mermet' (1869), a once-popular florist rose with elegant flesh pink buds and stiff stems; 'Maman Cochet' (1893), combining cream, pink, and rosy red in long-pointed buds; 'Rosette Delizy', with yellow petals edged and flushed in red. Two fine climbing teas are the creamy white 'Sombreuil' (1856), full of petals in a cupped to flat bloom; and 'Gloire de Dijon' (1853), the full, cupped flowers buff orange fading to creamy yellow and tinged with pink.

19th century development

The collection assembled at Malmaison contained rose species and natural hybrids other than those mentioned above, but from five of those mentioned—gallicas, damasks, centifolias, Chinas, and teas—the family group was assembled which would, in the span of less than 100 years, revolutionize the rose.

Until the time of Josephine, the development of new roses was largely in the hands of Mother Nature. Now and then a mutation would occur on an established sort, but planting seeds was by far the most common means of obtaining new roses. The species and their varieties contained enough inherent variability so that it was not uncommon for seedlings to differ (slightly to considerably) in appearance from their seed parent. If two different roses grew side by side (a gallica next to a damask, for example), it was always possible that some of the seeds taken from either one might have resulted from the pollen of the other—a true hybrid cross.

Empress Josephine's great contribution was to assemble for the first time in one place a large number of roses with widely different characteristics from widely separated geographical regions—roses that Mother Nature could never have brought together on her own. With the influx of new roses, distinctly different roses began cropping up in seedling plantings: hybrids between European and Chinese sorts. Moreover, Josephine made these roses available to hybridizers for their experiments. The new combinations found in these seedlings fired the imaginations of horticulturists, botanists, nurserymen, and gardeners alike. The resulting rose industry made France the leading rose-producing nation for over a century. More and more seeds were sown annually, resulting in rapid development of several new types of roses during the 19th century—and culminating in the first hybrid teas which have come to dominate 20th century rose gardens.

Noisette roses. While Josephine was building her collection at Malmaison, John Champneys, a rice planter in Charleston, South Carolina, raised a hybrid between 'Parson's Pink China' and the old autumn-blooming musk rose. The hybrid, which he named 'Champneys' Pink Cluster', was a vigorous climber producing huge clusters of small blush pink flowers from early spring until frost. Champneys' neighbor, Philippe Noisette, scion of a prominent French nursery family, planted seeds of Champneys' hybrid and sent the progeny to his brother in France. In 1818, 'Blush Noisette' was introduced and bestowed its name on a new class of climbing roses—the sole American contribution to the 19th century parade of new hybrid types.

The early Noisette roses were small-flowered, fairly hardy, shrubby climbers with the constant bloom of the China roses, in colors from white through pink to crimson and purple. European hybridizers crossed these small Noisettes with the larger-flowered tea roses, obtaining roses with larger blossoms in an expanded color range of yellow, salmon, and orange, but with smaller clusters and considerably reduced hardiness. These large-flowered tea-Noisettes are vigorous climbers suitable only to the warmer regions.

Noisettes contributed to modern roses on two fronts. Rather far back in the ancestry of the shrub roses known as hybrid musks (see page 24), the Noisettes furnished the source of the musk rose. More importantly, Noisettes entered into development of yellow tea roses and thence into later hybrid teas.

True Noisette roses are seldom sold now, but several climbing tea-Noisettes are still popular. Most famous is the lemon yellow 'Maréchal Niel' (1864), with buds of hybrid tea quality on slim stems that let them hang down toward the viewer. 'Madame Alfred Carriere' (1879) has double white blossoms, lightly flushed pink.

Portland roses. Emerging around 1800, this was the first new group of hybrids between the old European roses and the new Chinese introductions. Although their ancestries vary, all apparently were derived from at least the autumn damasks and the Chinas. Sometimes catalogued as damask perpetuals, they were almost always called Portland roses after their first representative, 'Duchess of Portland.' To roses that offered some hope of repeat bloom, the best of these brought rich red tones from China and gallica, combined with increased doubleness from centifolias. For about fifty years they maintained some popularity until they were eclipsed by their own descendants, the hybrid perpetuals (see page 14).

Few Portland roses are now available, but among those few are the following three, all compact plants with intensely fragrant, full-petaled blossoms: 'Comte de Chambord' (1860), rich pink; 'Jacques Cartier' (1868), clear light pink; and 'Rose du Roi' (1815), rich red with both lighter and darker tones intermingled.

Bourbon roses. Having nothing to do with Kentucky, Bourbon roses had their origin, instead, on the Isle of Bourbon (now Réunion) in the Indian Ocean off Madagascar. Cultivated fields on the island often were fenced with mixed hedges of roses, particularly including 'Parson's Pink China' and the autumn damask. In 1819, a visiting French botanist discovered in one hedge a seedling which was an obvious hybrid between these two roses. He sent seeds from it back to King Louis Philippe's gardener in Paris. From that seed came the original Bourbon rose—a semi-double deep pink that flowered repeatedly. Its plants were vigorous semi-climbers with large, shiny green leaves and purple-tinted canes. Many Bourbon hybrids were named and sold during the 1800s, the best of which retained the Bourbon foliage and plant characteristics, as well as the repeat flowering. Ironically, the important old Bourbon-China hybrid 'Gloire des Rosomanes'—one of the primary sources of red color in today's hybrid teas—has persisted in countless gardens today, but as an understock for modern roses!

Nineteenth-century Bourbons sold today include 'Honorine de Brabant', globular to cupped flowers of blush pink irregularly striped in darker tones verging on violet; 'Souvenir de la Malmaison' (1843), both bush and climbing forms, flesh pink flowers full of petals opening cup-shaped and expanding to flat; 'Reine Victoria' (1872) and its sport 'Madame Pierre Oger' (1878), both with rounded blossoms of shell-shaped petals, the former a deep rose pink, the latter a creamy flesh pink deepening in sunshine. 'Madame Isaac Pereire' (1880) and its sport 'Madame Ernst Calvat' (1888) feature big, cupped flowers with penetrating fragrance—magenta pink and rich flesh pink, respectively—on husky plants that can be either large shrubs or small climbers. 'Zephirine Drouhin' (1868), semi-double bright cerise pink, is a restrained climber noted for its absence of thorns.

(Continued on page 14)

Reine Victoria (Bourbon)

Rose du Roi (Portland)   *Hermosa* (China)

The Chinese Influence

Introduction of the China rose into western Europe dramatically transformed garden roses in the 19th century. Not only did it alter flower style and plant growth habits, but, most importantly, it brought into these new hybrid classes its capacity for flowering more than once a year. The stage was set for the emergence of our "modern" roses.

Catherine Mermet (Tea)

Mrs. John Laing (Hybrid Perpetual)   *The Fairy* (Polyantha)

Sources for Old Roses

Collecting old roses is something of an adventure because they are generally not available except from a growing band of specialized mail-order nurseries. Many of these have tapped European old rose sources and have brought some truly historic as well as attractive roses back into cultivation. The following nurseries offer representative old roses of all classes.

Roses of Yesterday and Today (catalog $2.00)
802 Brown's Valley Road
Watsonville, CA 95076

The Antique Rose Emporium (catalog $2.00)
Route 5, Box 143
Brenham, TX 77833

Harrison's Antique & Modern Roses, Inc.
(catalog $2.00)
P.O. Box 527
Canton, MS 39046

Heritage Rose Gardens (catalog $2.00)
16831 Mitchell Creek Drive
Fort Bragg, CA 95437

Devotees of old roses formed the Heritage Roses Group so that they might share their enthusiasm, experiences, and even their roses. For a small annual membership fee you can receive their informative quarterly, "The Rose Letter." Send inquiries to Patricia Cole, Drawer K, Mesilla, NM 88046.

You can still find many old roses thriving in cemeteries and in old or abandoned farmsteads. Most of these old roses grow easily from cuttings, so you can add these nameless survivors to your garden. Follow the directions for cuttings on pages 92–93.

Hybrid perpetuals. The first roses that could be classed as hybrid perpetuals made their appearance around 1838. From then until just after the turn of the century, the production of these roses occupied all rose breeders of any consequence; the result was more than three thousand of them before their offspring, the hybrid teas (see this page), pushed them out of the gardens. They were the 19th century garden and cut flower workhorses, particularly in regions where the teas would not thrive.

Hybrids they definitely were, encompassing in their ancestries practically all garden roses that had gone before them; but many were far from perpetual—in the sense of Chinas and teas. The tendency was for a massive spring flowering followed by scattered bloom for the rest of the year, or by a smaller fall burst, or—by nothing. Colors ranged from white through all shades of pink and red to purple, generally in large, full-petaled flowers. Most were capable of forming large plants, often with long, almost climbing canes that produced their best flowers (and their greatest quantity of them) when "pegged down" into a low arch. Several red hybrid Chinas (among them 'Gloire des Rosomanes') and the dark red Portland rose 'Rose du Roi' are supposed to be chiefly responsible for the red shades in the group.

As the hybrid teas gained in numbers, the hybrid perpetuals lost favor because of three handicaps: limited color range, lack of a dependable perpetual-flowering inclination, and rampant growth habit. But in comparison to more modern roses, blooms of the best old hybrid perpetuals don't take a back seat.

A number of hybrid perpetuals have survived to the present day in catalogs. Among those with pink flowers are 'Baronne Prévost' (1842), 'Baroness Rothschild' (1868), 'Paul Neyron' (1869), with huge, "cabbage rose"-style blossoms, 'Mrs. John Laing' (1887), 'Georg Arends' (1910), 'Heinrich Münch' (1911), and 'Arrillaga' (1929). Dark reds include the famous 'Général Jacqueminot' (1853), an ancestor of nearly all modern red roses, and 'Henry Nevard' (1924); lighter reds are 'Ulrich Brunner fils' (1882) and 'Hugh Dickson' (1905). White-edged red petals are found on 'Roger Lambelin' (1890) and 'Baron Girod de l'Ain' (1897); 'Ferdinand Pichard' (1921) has petals striped in red and pink shades. Purple, violet, and lilac tones combine in 'Reine des Violettes' (1860). The best known in modern gardens is the snow white 'Frau Karl Druschki' (1901).

Modern roses

Anything to which the term "modern" is applied inevitably becomes obsolete in time. To rose growers, however, "modern" began in 1867 with the introduction of what is designated as the first hybrid tea—and this is the class of roses that still dominates present day rose gardens.

Hybrid teas. These did not come on the rose scene with great fanfare. In fact, they crept in so imperceptibly that there is some question as to which really was the first hybrid tea. The general formula is hybrid perpetual x tea rose; but because the planting of naturally pollinated seed was common practice throughout the 19th century, many notable roses have ancestries traceable only on the maternal side (or not at all when hips were gathered at random). Since the hybrid perpetuals were such a melting pot of other roses, a few do show evidence of tea rose background.

The designation of 'La France' (1867) as the first hybrid tea, however, marked the beginning of a new era in roses.

To determine early hybrid teas, the best guide is their growth and flowering habits. They usually grow on smaller but bushier plants than the hybrid perpetuals, and they are almost everblooming in all climates. Until 1900, the color range in this new class was the same as that found among the hybrid perpetuals, with the addition of creamy yellow tints from the teas. Of the 19th century hybrid teas in addition to 'La France', two stand out. 'Mme. Caroline Testout' was a very popular pink because of its beauty and adaptability; it is the rose that once was planted by the thousands along the streets of Portland, Oregon. The other is 'Kaiserin Auguste Viktoria', still an excellent white in climates where its many-petaled flowers can open well. Two early 20th century hybrid teas belong to this select group of old favorites. Bright pink 'Radiance' has been beloved for its ability to grow well in nearly all rose-growing areas. 'Ophelia' is renowned for its perfect form and its contribution as a parent to modern roses.

The year 1900 was a revolutionary turning point for hybrid teas in particular and, indeed, for roses in general: it marked the introduction of Joseph Pernet's 'Soleil d'Or'. Derived from a purple-red hybrid perpetual and 'Persian Yellow' (a double form of the Austrian brier rose, *Rosa foetida*), this was the first large, deep yellow, reasonably hardy bush rose. Up to that time, some tea roses were yellow-flowered, but they were tender plants, their yellow very quickly fading to nearly white. While not strictly a hybrid tea, 'Soleil d'Or' ("Golden Sun") did remarkable things when crossed with one. Suddenly an entirely new palette of colors emerged: bright golden yellow, flame, copper, soft orange, and bicolors of yellow and almost any other color. This was like a transfusion to the tired blood of white, pink, and red-flowered roses. There was, however, a price to pay for the exotic new colors. From *Rosa foetida* these new hybrids inherited a tendency toward poorly-formed blooms (the easiest fault to overcome in later hybridizing), lustrous foliage that was particularly susceptible to black spot, and a resentment of pruning—followed by die-back if their canes were severely cut back, either by design or harsh winters. For a number of years, these roses formed a separate sub-class called pernetianas, but by the 1930s they had been crossed so extensively with hybrid teas that the latter group absorbed them. The glorious pernetiana colors have permeated all modern rose classes, but so has the hidden legacy of their dislike for pruning shears. Curiously enough, the lavender, mauve, russet, and gray tones that have cropped up in modern roses are not just derived from the purple-toned hybrid perpetuals, but are also a result of interaction with the bright pernetiana colors.

Polyanthas and floribundas. The earliest polyantha roses, derived from the Japanese *Rosa multiflora* and forms of *Rosa chinensis*, made their appearance in France at about the same time as the hybrid teas. Typically, a polyantha blossoms continually on short, compact plants. Blooms are about an inch across, of no special form, but in large clusters that may cover the plant. Two early polyantha hybrids, 'Cecile Brunner' (1880) and 'Perle d'Or' (1883) have maintained their popularity to this day. They, too, flower in large clusters but have the added feature of shapely blooms on considerably larger plants. The ranunculus-like, salmon orange 'Margo Koster' and soft pink 'The Fairy' are later representatives of the type.

A number of other species entered into ancestries of roses classed as polyanthas after 1900. The continuous production of large clusters of small flowers on low plants was the determining factor in the polyantha classification.

Inevitably, these cluster-flowering polyantha types were crossed with hybrid teas to gain better form, increased color range, and still larger flowers on a profuse plant. Some records indicate that the first of these was the floribunda 'Gruss an Aachen', raised from seed of 'Frau Karl Druschki' and introduced in 1909. But for intentional development of this new rose type by crossing hybrid teas with polyanthas, the Poulsen family in Denmark were pioneers. They hoped to obtain hardiness and freedom of flowering from the polyantha types. It soon became evident, however, that the new hybrids from this union would need some designation other than polyantha, or even hybrid polyantha. The larger flowers and shrubbier plants definitely set them apart from the polyantha category. Finally, in the 1940s, the term "floribunda" was coined for the class.

Ever since the first of the type was developed, floribundas have been undergoing a continuing transition through repeated crossings with hybrid teas. From the single or semi-double, rather informal blossoms in large clusters typical of early floribundas, you now have floribundas in all the hybrid tea colors with the best hybrid tea flower form. In some cases, blooms have become so large and clusters so small that a hybrid tea classification is almost justified.

Grandifloras. The hybrid tea-floribunda hybrids which fit neither category were designated grandifloras. Although the name often has been challenged (British rosarians refer to those roses as "floribundas, hybrid tea type"), it is fairly descriptive of the type.

They *are* grand. The plants usually are larger and more vigorous than the average hybrid tea. Flowers may be as large as hybrid teas but they are borne on fairly long stems within few-flowered clusters; consequently they approach floribunda bloom production. The standard for the class is still 'Queen Elizabeth', with her clusters of large, rather informal flowers on a rugged, skyscraping plant. Some hybrid teas have been reclassified to grandiflora because of their vigor and tendency to bloom in small clusters. On

Ophelia

20th Century Progress

Rosa foetida bicolor ("Austrian Copper")

The hybrid teas have dominated 20th century rose gardens, and one of the most influential in modern rose development has been 'Ophelia' (1912). Addition of *Rosa foetida* (here represented by its color form "Austrian Copper") to the basic hybrid tea made possible the current yellow, orange, and flame-colored roses. Polyantha combined with hybrid tea produced the floribunda, first of which was 'Gruss an Aachen' (1909). By bringing untried species into breeding programs, new developments are possible: 'Picasso' is the first of a new color pattern; 'Thérèse Bugnet' is exceptionally winter-hardy.

Thérèse Bugnet

Picasso

Pink Gruss an Aachen

the other hand, some grandifloras ('Mount Shasta', for example) might as well be hybrid teas, for their flowers are as shapely as any and often come one to a stem.

Miniature roses. There were miniature forms of all the old European rose types—gallicas, damasks, albas, centifolias, even mosses. They were popular in the 18th century but lapsed into neglect after the introduction of the miniature China rose. Exact origin of this rose, *Rosa chinensis minima,* is clouded, but the first plants reached Europe shortly after 1800—apparently from the island of Mauritius, a British possession in the Indian Ocean.

Miniatures have gone through two widely separated periods of development—first in the years 1820–1850, then in the years after 1930. Development of polyantha roses (see page 15) eclipsed the popularity of miniature roses in the last century, but rediscovery, around 1920 in Switzerland, of an attractive miniature growing profusely in window boxes again awakened interest in the type. To gain an increased color range and finer flower form, hybridizers have crossed floribundas and polyanthas with miniatures. The result is some variation in miniature size, but perfect replicas of modern hybrid tea flowers. More recently, crossing miniature roses with climbing roses of *Rosa wichuraiana* derivation has produced a series of climbing miniatures.

ROSES OF THE FUTURE

Just as the 19th century saw the rise of hybrid perpetuals and tea roses, and then—at its end—saw them gradually give way to their offspring, the hybrid teas, there is no reason to expect the current hybrid teas not to evolve into still another type of rose that will embody their virtues and bring new ones as well.

New colors, improved plants

Previously unused, or underexplored, rose species will find their ways into future roses as hybridizers quest for new colors and patterns (remembering what *Rosa foetida* did to the hybrid tea color range) and pursue two utopian goals: disease-proof foliage and completely winter-hardy plants.

From Ireland's (now New Zealand's) Sam McGredy IV have come a group of floribundas dubbed the "hand-painted series" ('Picasso' was the first introduced). The group features flowers of red and white, with the red appearing brushed onto the petals and leaving a white central "eye." In their ancestry is the Scotch brier, *Rosa spinosissima,* a species seldom used except in production of large shrub roses. They serve, in a small way, to show what is possible when a hybridizer reaches beyond the usual

hybrid tea/floribunda melting pot.

Better plant qualities are more difficult to achieve. Disease-resistant foliage is nothing new—many teas have it, as do *Rosa rugosa* and its varieties, and the rampant climber 'Mermaid'. But the quality becomes lost in hybridizing (as with rugosas), carries with it the liability of tenderness (as with the teas), or is difficult to explore because of near-sterility as with 'Mermaid'.

The ability of a rose plant to survive sub-zero winters with no protection and little or no damage to canes has been sought for decades by hybridizers in Europe, Canada, and the United States. Various species exist that have these qualities; the problem is to transfer them to a plant that bears flowers of hybrid tea beauty.

The most progress has come from Wilhelm Kordes in Germany and Griffith Buck in Iowa. From an artificially created "species," *Rosa kordesii,* Kordes has bred a series of shrub and climbing roses that are hardier than the average hybrid tea.

The Buck hybrids more nearly approach modern hybrid teas and floribundas in growth and flower. As a group, they stem from earlier Kordes species hybrids, several grandifloras, *Rosa wichuraiana,* and *Rosa laxa* from central Asia. But progress on hardiness is beset by the same difficulties as is breeding for better foliage.

It is certain, though, with geneticists and knowledgeable hybridizers working toward the ultimate foolproof rose, that roses will improve faster than they did in the early 19th century when rosarians sowed naturally formed hips and *hoped* for some exciting differences.

New classification system

As rose hybridizers continue to strive toward new goals, the products of their work become increasingly difficult to pigeonhole into current classes such as hybrid tea, grandiflora, and floribunda. Recognizing the present terms' inadequacies, the World Federation of Rose Societies is promoting a new classification system for all roses (except old garden roses) based upon flower and plant styles and growth habits. Our modern roses first would be divided according to growth—climbing or non-climbing—and then each of these classes divided between repeat-flowering and once-blooming. The non-climbing/repeat-flowering category, in which most popular bush roses fall, would be further separated into five types: shrub roses; large-flowered bush roses that have shapely individual blossoms on long cutting stems (with or without side buds); cluster-flowered roses that have smaller, often less shapely, flowers but a profusion of them; polyantha roses (same as existing class); and miniature roses.

Worldwide adoption of the new classification will be some years in coming. Its eventual implementation, however, should be welcomed by gardeners and rosarians alike.

Roses in Your Landscape

Virtually no other popular garden ornamental comes close to matching the versatility of the rose. Its use in your garden really is limited by only three factors: suitability of your garden for roses in general, your garden's size, and your imagination.

Stated in clinical terms, a rose is a flowering shrub. But remarkable shrub it is, encompassing a great variety of growth types and foliage and flower forms, a wide range of colors, a long flowering season, decorative fruits, and nearly limitless combinations of these variables. Do you need a bedding plant that will flower almost continually yet never need replanting? Then choose one of the miniatures or a lower growing floribunda. Even some of the low hybrid teas can serve this purpose.

You can plan hedges of any size and description: low and profuse with floribundas, polyanthas, or miniatures; high and showy with grandifloras; or informal and nearly impenetrable with some of the shrub varieties and species. Miniature roses—perfect replicas of modern hybrid teas and floribundas—can border a planting of larger roses or other flowers, as well as grow in containers either indoors or outside.

Fences, walls, arbors, and trellises traditionally are strongholds of rose display, but a number of those that you train up and over also will grow down and out—as ground or slope covers. The showy orange fruits or "hips" on some climbers and shrub types provide a splash of autumn color that rivals the beauty of the spring bloom.

Shrub roses, left to go their own exuberant ways with a minimum of trimming, can provide a backdrop to other rose plantings, at the same time tying the entire plan together because of the similar foliage and flowers. Some of the repeat-flowering shrub roses easily could replace other flowering shrubs, such as lilacs, that bloom but once each year.

Rose growing need not be limited to the open garden. For close-up enjoyment, bring them onto your patio or terrace. Floribundas and miniatures are tailor-made for small patio planting areas or raised beds; the shelter from wind or winter cold provided there also may be what is needed to bring out the best in one of the repeat-flowering climbers. And don't overlook the value of roses in large containers. Any of the newer miniatures or floribundas with hybrid tealike flowers (or some of the shorter hybrid teas themselves) can become beautiful conversation pieces when displayed this way. In containers you can easily give them the regular watering, fertilizing, and close individual attention that will encourage them to perform to perfection. See pages 91-92 for details of growing roses in containers.

Not only your choice of roses but also how you use them can influence the mood of your garden picture. Evenly spaced plants in geometrically shaped rose beds present a more formal, organized look—the precision of a military formation with the beauty of a chorus line. The same roses used in flowing curves and irregularly shaped planting areas appear more casual, relaxed, informal, or "natural." A row of standards, whether straight or curving, will give direction to the eye and to anyone strolling through the garden, but just one can provide *emphasis*. A single, well-groomed standard—strategically placed—or just one pillar rose can be as eye-catching as a bed of mixed varieties.

Many more examples could be cited, but they all center around one point: roses in general are a highly varied group of shrubs, and their usefulness, even among the most widely grown types, extends far beyond the traditional "rose bed" concept.

Before you decide to plant any kind of rose, first consider what roses need in order to flourish. Then you can place them wherever in your garden they are most likely to succeed.

(Continued on page 23)

LIVING TAPESTRY OF ROSES decorates garden and house. Climbing roses are 'Handel' and 'America', while prominent floribunda in foreground is 'Cathedral'.

Featuring Roses in the Landscape

A few photographs illustrate better than words some of the many garden uses of various modern roses. *Opposite page:* 'Climbing Cecile Brunner' (left) smothers arbor in bounty of perfectly formed pastel pink blossoms. Rambler roses, as well as climbing floribundas and polyanthas, will give a similarly lavish display. A more traditional rose bed of hybrid teas and grandifloras (lower left) is edged with low-growing floribundas; polyanthas and larger-growing miniatures could provide the same colorful edging. Polyantha 'Margo Koster' (right) assorts with gerberas of similar color in mixed border planting. *This page:* Climbing 'Royal Sunset' (top right) shows mass of bloom when canes are trained horizontally. 'Americana' (lower left) demonstrates garden impact produced by just one well-grown specimen in a container. Mixed landscape planting of annuals and perennials (lower right) features one white tea rose that has been allowed to build up into a large background shrub.

Kathleen

Rosa rugosa rubra

Kathleen, autumn hips

Shrub Roses

Illustrated here are examples of the various shrub rose types described on pages 24 and 25. Garden value is based not on beauty of individual blossoms but on the mass display of blossoms on plants that are rugged, easy to grow, and clothed in disease-resistant, often attractive foliage.

Harison's Yellow

Pink Grootendorst

Belinda

WHERE TO GROW ROSES

A rose's requirements are not difficult to understand or to satisfy. Ignoring them, however, means risking disappointment and doing an injustice to a beautiful flower. By keeping the following points in mind when planning locations for your roses, you should be rewarded by years of increasing pleasure as your roses prosper.

• Roses, once planted, do not like to be disturbed often and are a greater chore to move as years pass and plants become larger. Plan ahead.

• Roses like sun and require it to flourish. See that they receive it for at least 6 hours each day, preferably in the morning. In cool or frequently overcast climates they'll do best if planted where they can receive sunshine all day. In regions having intense summer heat, plant roses where they'll be shaded from the scorching glare and heat of afternoon sun; filtered shade cast by high trees growing at some distance from the roses is good. (Roses will *grow* in shade. But plants there usually are disappointingly leggy with sparse bloom—while mildew and rust are more troublesome and more difficult to control.)

• Avoid planting roses in windswept places. Strong or continuous winds spoil flowers and cause excessive transpiration from leaves so that you have to water more often than normally would be needed.

• Roses like the soil to themselves (shrub roses excepted—see page 24). Be wary of planting near trees and shrubs: their roots have an insidious habit of reaching into rose beds and stealing a good portion of the better supply of water and nutrients there.

• Rose soil must drain well, though it should be moisture retentive.

When planning where to plant your roses, keep in mind the added enjoyment you can have if they are visible from inside the house.

Another point you might tuck away in the back of your mind is an expansion plan. Your first success with roses often will whet your appetite to grow more, and each year brings alluring new varieties to add to your garden. If you can, allow ground room for expansion of your first plantings.

Layout

After you select a place for roses, your next concern will be the garden layout. With so many attractive varieties available, you may be tempted to buy whatever looks interesting and then crowd them all into a big, sunny bed. The best advice, if you are in danger of succumbing, is *don't*. If you realize that all roses probably will need some fertilizing, pruning, and occasional attention to pest control, you'll understand the value of planning for easy maintenance.

The wide, deep, and crowded rose bed will become in a few years a colorful thicket which will only discourage you from giving plants the attention they deserve.

Plantings that you can reach from at least two sides are the easiest to care for. Make sure your rose bed is just wide enough that plants in the center can be reached from either side. This makes it easy for you to perform all routine maintenance without walking through the roses and compacting the soil around them. If you plant in a bed that abuts a fence or wall, your work will be simpler if the planting is two, or at the most three, bushes deep. You'll also find if you plant in parallel rows, staggered spacing makes for easier maintenance.

If your intended rose bed will be bordered by lawn, you can do two things to make the unavoidable edging task easier. First, plan for as few beds as possible; this cuts down on the number of feet of edges you'll have to trim. Second, a brick, concrete, concrete block, or wood mowing strip between lawn and bed will keep the bed edge even and simplify mowing right up to the edge.

As you spend pleasant hours selecting roses for your intended garden, look past the glowing color descriptions and check for information on growth habits. It's crucial to choose the right roses for your plan. A rampant, 30-foot climber will be entirely unsuited to a 10-foot-wide patio wall, for example, whereas a climber of moderate growth or a pillar rose would suit the landscape admirably. Similarly, don't put a modest little bush like 'Picture' behind a robust giant like 'Queen Elizabeth': you'll never see it.

Spacing

How far apart you plant your roses depends upon your climate and the particular roses you plant. Where winter cold forces you to prune down to 1 to 2 feet each spring and the following growing season is short, bushes seldom achieve the bulk that they do in warmer regions. Planted 24 to 30 inches apart, hybrid teas and grandifloras will fill in the bed well without becoming tangled. Throughout most of the South, Southwest, and West, hybrid teas and grandifloras normally will go about 36 inches apart. Where there is little or no frost to force definite winter dormancy (such as in parts of Southern California, the Gulf Coast, and Florida), rose bushes grow so prodigiously all year that they need to be planted up to 48 inches or more apart.

Most floribundas generally are smaller but bushier plants, and are massed in plantings for group effect. Except for especially vigorous, spreading varieties, space them about 24 inches apart in colder climates and 30 inches apart where winters are relatively mild.

Most shrub roses and many "old garden roses" need more elbow room than modern hybrids, but just how much depends upon the growth habit of the varieties or species you intend to plant. From 5 to 6 feet apart is a reasonable guide, perhaps a little more for any varieties whose canes you plan to peg down in order to get bloom all along their length (see page 87).

SHRUB ROSES, OLD AND MODERN

Up to this point, landscaping advice has been aimed at planting rose beds because the majority of gardeners choose this sort of planting. But roses as flowering shrubs are receiving more and more attention. Why plant a lilac or buddleia, for example, when you can plant a rose? The once-blooming sorts can be just as bountiful and colorful as other spring or summer-flowering shrubs, and if you choose a repeat-blooming kind you can spread color through two or three seasons. In addition to flower color, some roses set quantities of decorative hips which can liven the landscape in fall and winter.

A great many of the old garden roses discussed on pages 6–14 are best used as flowering shrubs, planted where they have elbow room to spread. Especially among the gallicas, albas, centifolias, Chinas, teas, Portlands, and Bourbons, you will find varieties that are first-rate shrub roses. Of those types, the last four are repeat-flowering.

But besides the old garden roses there are other classes that contain admirable shrubs. Some are old roses that did not enter the mainstream of development; some are mixed-ancestry hybrids that fit no particular classification; others are 20th century products, the results of deliberate attempts to create shrub roses that will embody the colors or refinement of flower form of hybrid teas. The following paragraphs present these various types and mention some outstanding varieties to try. In general, their availability is more limited than the modern garden roses charted on pages 27–61; growers of old garden roses (see page 14) are likely sources.

Hybrid musks. These are only remotely related to the old autumn-flowering musk rose through the Noisette roses (see page 11), and some may not be able to claim even that tenuous link. Nevertheless, these are mostly vigorous, well-foliaged bushes 4–8 feet high and wide, with clustered, highly fragrant blossoms in the style of many floribundas. They are repeat-flowering, but best displays are spring and fall; some form good clusters of hips for winter display (see photos of 'Kathleen' on page 22). Foliage is notably disease resistant, and most plants will perform well in partly shaded locations as well as in full sun. Among the better and more widely sold hybrid musks are 'Belinda', bright pink, 1-inch, semi-double blooms in large clusters; 'Buff Beauty', creamy apricot buff, very double flowers (in the fashion of some old garden roses), bronzy new growth and arching canes; 'Cornelia', small rosette-shaped flowers of coral pink fading to creamy pink; 'Kathleen', blush pink, appleblossom-style blooms, each about half-dollar size, on a very vigorous bush; 'Penelope', salmon orange buds, fluffy semi-double, creamy buff 3-inch blossoms—and winter hips of coral pink color; 'Will Scarlet', semi-double bluish scarlet blooms, glossy orange red hips in winter.

Rugosas. In this group are forms of the species *Rosa rugosa*, and hybrids of the species with other types. "Rugose" means "rutted" and describes the foliage: characteristically ribbed and veined and in the species, diseaseproof. In summer-rainfall areas and maritime climates, the species is drought-tolerant and will grow in practically pure sand in the salt spray of the seashore. Big, tomato-colored hips follow the blooms; and since most are repeat-flowering, hips and flowers may intermingle. Habit is rounded, dense, and covered with leaves that will turn yellow in autumn. Plants are very winter hardy without protection. Various forms of the species may be sold, including 'Alba', single white flowers; 'Rosea', single bluish pink flowers; 'Rubra', not red, but a dark wine pink. Rugosa hybrids are 'Belle Poitevine', a tall shrub with double lilac pink blooms to 4 inches followed by good hips; 'Blanc Double de Coubert', pure white and semi-double, red hips, the foliage less dense than the species; 'F. J. Grootendorst' (and its sports 'Grootendorst Supreme' and 'Pink Grootendorst'), small clustered blossoms resembling carnations because petal edges are deeply fringed; 'Fru Dagmar Hastrup', pure light pink, single flowers and crimson red hips; 'Hansa', another taller plant with vivid purplish-red, double flowers and red hips; 'Roseraie de l'Haÿ', long, pointed buds opening to loosely double blooms in a brighter tone of purplish red than in 'Hansa'; 'Will Alderman', semi-double lilac pink blooms followed by tomato red hips.

Miscellaneous modern shrubs. Unlike the roses in the previous two groups, these roses are such individuals that most of them cannot be grouped with others of similar characteristics and origin. A Baker's Dozen might include these:

'Constance Spry', restrained climbing habit, best used against wall or fence, although can be pruned as free-standing shrub; large, full, cupped, rich pink flowers in the old rose style, in one spring bloom period.

'Frühlingsgold', a big, arching bush, its branches laden in spring with 5-inch, nearly single, creamy yellow, fragrant flowers.

'Frühlingsmorgen', a slightly smaller bush than 'Frühlingsgold' and bearing a heavy spring show of 4-inch, single blossoms—rose pink with yellow centers and maroon anthers; may give a smaller crop of flowers in late summer.

'Goldbusch', a spreading shrub or restrained climber, dark coral-colored buds open to fairly double blooms of buff yellow to cream; produces two crops of flowers per year.

'Golden Wings', single or nearly single bright, light yellow flowers with contrasting red brown stamens; upright, tall growth.

'Gruss an Teplitz', a medium-height, spreading bush, usually with small clusters of rich, dark crimson double blossoms having a fine fragrance and coming throughout the blooming season; good for hedging.

'Harison's Yellow', circa 1830—so not really modern—but historically important because it was carried west by the pioneers; fernlike foliage on a fairly sparse bush, with a spring flowering of bright yellow, 3-inch semi-double blossoms; quite drought tolerant when established.

'Hon. Lady Lindsay', flowers of hybrid tea form in soft salmon pink; medium-height plant is bushy, spreading, with glossy, leathery foliage.

'Nevada', a tall, spreading shrub magnificent when covered in its 4-inch, semi-double, creamy white blossoms; the spring bloom is lavish, smaller bursts occur throughout the season. (A pink sport is 'Marguerite Hilling'.)

'Nymphenburg' makes a loose bush and a better restrained climber or pillar; the clustered, double, and fragrant blooms combine salmon pink and orange, with tinges of pink and yellow.

'Poulsen's Park Rose', pale pink hybrid-tea-like blooms are clustered on a spreading, full bush clothed in shiny, bronze-tinted foliage.

'Sparrieshoop', a big, voluptuous shrub or moderate climber, the flowers appearing like bright pink butterflies—ruffled and basically single—throughout the year; bronze new growth, bronze-tinted foliage.

'Thérèse Bugnet', double flowers of lilac pink opening from nearly red buds have a fluffy, informal quality; developed in Canada to withstand winters there with no protection.

Grandifloras. Although a modern rose category (currently popular varieties are described in the color categories found on pages 27–61), the most vigorous of these roses will function as freestanding shrubs and as background hedges. Among the best for these purposes are 'Carrousel' (red), 'Queen Elizabeth' (pink), 'Arizona' (orange), and 'Sundowner' (orange).

COLOR HARMONY

Some gardeners feel that all nature's colors combine pleasantly. But if the idea of a screaming orange 'Tropicana' next to the deep, cold pink of 'Miss All-American Beauty' makes you grit your teeth, then you'll want to give some thought to establishing a good-neighbor color policy in your rose bed.

Strong colors. Colors that need the greatest care in placement are the pure, unshaded, full tones: clear

American Rose Society

In 1899, the American Rose Society was founded to unite—via the printed word—the many individuals interested in roses, to spread information on all aspects of rose growing, and to foster research. Today, the ARS holds two national conventions a year and prints a monthly magazine as well as an annual publication of 200 or more pages. Each annual carries a "Proof of the Pudding" feature: a compilation of nationwide evaluations of the newer rose varieties. Each year, too, the society prints a pamphlet that gives point-score ratings of all roses currently grown in the United States; the ratings derive from surveys of the national membership. For membership details and current subscription fee, write to: The American Rose Society, P.O. Box 30,000, Shreveport, LA 71130.

To provide aid to new members of ARS, as well as general information at the local level, the American Rose Society established the Consulting Rosarian program—a countrywide network of dedicated and experienced rose growers who have volunteered to give advice on rose culture and selection pertinent to their areas. Beyond such advice, they can also put you in touch with any local, regional, or state society, through which you might expand your fund of rose lore in the fellowship of other keen rose growers.

orange and orange scarlet, bright red, deep yellow, and dark pink. The even orange of 'Tropicana' is more difficult to harmonize than the blended orange-copper of 'Mojave', for example, because 'Tropicana', being entirely one shade, almost always contrasts with its neighbors, whereas a yellow blend may pick up some of the paler orange tones of 'Mojave' and tie the two together. Some dazzling contrasts can be established by placing some of the pure, bright colors side by side (such as yellow next to red or orange), but too much of this assaults the eye rather than pleases it. You also can use white roses to contrast with these bright, clear colors.

Soft colors. The easiest colors to mix throughout your rose plantings are cream, buff, light yellow, yellow blends, pink blends, and yellow and pink combinations. These can act as buffers for the strong colors and intercede between unrelated colors to tie them together. The soft yellow and pink of 'Peace', for example, can step in between magenta and orange varieties to prevent an otherwise strong clash. The lavender and mauve roses associate well with these soft and blended colors, as well as with the dark, rich reds and most deep yellows.

A Shopper's List of Favorite Roses

Since color is the primary factor in most people's choices of roses, the descriptions and photographs through page 61 are arranged in color groups to give you a comparative idea of varieties of similar color. Such careful organization, however, is challenged by the roses which do not always accept easy pigeonholing. Red is red—but when you view blackish 'Oklahoma' beside orange scarlet 'Olé' you begin to get an idea of the complexities involved and the judgments that had to be made in order to present the varieties in color groups. The greatest challenge was in separating pink from orange from multicolor. Precisely where salmon pink leaves off and light orange begins may be a matter of individual eye. To confound the viewer even further, the intensity of color—the degree of orangeness or redness—can vary according to the weather. The creamy pink 'Michele Meilland', for example, will vary from that color through salmon pink to amber orange; but the predominant color for the majority of the bloom season was used to categorize the variety. Separating orange from multicolor was a matter of putting all solidly colored orange tones under orange, those which exhibit separately distinguishable colors under multicolor. But, under orange, you will find roses from light buff to bronzy ochre as well as shades of orange that fall between coral and red. Where a variety is listed as a "blend," it means that the colors shade from one into another; in contrast, a "bicolor" consists of two distinct colors—one on the inside, the other on the outside of the petals.

The following charts are grouped by color for the bush roses: hybrid tea, grandiflora, floribunda, and polyantha. Then come two pages of climbing roses listed alphabetically and two pages of miniature roses.

It is impractical to give absolute heights for the roses described—so much depends on climate, pruning, and general culture. But the relative sizes of low (L), medium (M), and tall (T) should hold in all regions; the tallest varieties in midwestern and eastern gardens also will be tallest in frost-free areas of the West and South.

The abbreviation AARS designates an All-America Rose Selection. In carefully supervised test gardens throughout the country, forthcoming introductions may be grown and evaluated over a two-year period. Only those roses that score high on all points of performance and appearance win the coveted AARS award. Since the first awards in 1940, the AARS designation has generally been an indication of roses that will be satisfactory in most parts of the country.

There is no better aid to rose selection than actually confronting the roses growing and blooming. Refer to pages 66–67 under "Which varieties to choose" for information on where to see roses.

One benefit of membership in the American Rose Society is the opportunity for personal contact with rose growers, often via local and district organizations (see page 25 for membership information). In your search for varieties that will give you the greatest satisfaction, the combination of seeing the roses and being able to talk about them with an experienced grower is unbeatable.

Roses as cut flowers. The bare-root bushes you buy in winter or early spring will have begun growth only two years earlier as understock cuttings or seedlings. These new plants will need the minimum of a year to become established in your garden before they can produce typical growth and bloom; and to establish well they will need all their foliage (see "How a plant grows" on page 83). Wait until their second spring in your garden before considering your roses as cut-flower sources.

For long-lasting cut roses, pick flowers in early morning or late afternoon, re-cut the stems under water, then plunge them into water up to the bases of the blooms. Leave all foliage on the stems: it absorbs water, too. Keep the blooms in a cool place overnight (if afternoon-picked) or for several hours (if cut in the morning), then arrange the flowers. Roses to be held overnight from afternoon picking should be cut in tighter bud than you want in your arrangement; they will fill out and expand during the night.

A RED, RED ROSE . . . to many, the embodiment of all the word "rose" implies. This is the 1984 AARS winner 'Olympiad' (see page 32).

Olé   Snowfire

Christian Dior   Mr. Lincoln

Europeana   Showbiz

Red Roses
velvet richness to jewel brightness

Chrysler Imperial

Sarabande   *Scarlet Knight*

Red Devil

...Red Roses

Frensham

Eye Paint

RED ROSES

NAME & TYPE	COLOR	HEIGHT	DESCRIPTION
AMERICANA Hybrid Tea	Crimson	M	Its good, high-centered form and profusion of bloom mark it as an ideal cut-flower variety. Color is rich medium red, noteworthy for lack of fading or bluing. Good fragrance.
AMERICAN PRIDE Hybrid Tea	Rich red	M	Deep red, ovoid buds spiral open to full, lightly fragrant double blossoms; petal edges recurve so that each petal becomes pointed, producing a starlike flower. Foliage is medium green, glossy.
CARROUSEL Grandiflora	Vivid dark red	T	Dark maroon red buds open to warm dark red blooms, some singly but more often in small clusters. Great for hedges or backgrounds: plants are vigorous, tall, and bushy.
CHRISTIAN DIOR Hybrid Tea (Photo on page 28)	Cherry red	T	AARS 1962. Elegant, blood red buds unfurl to slightly lighter red flowers that retain their attractiveness when fully open, and do not fade or blue. The outside of the petals is a little lighter and duller than the inside. No fragrance.
CHRYSLER IMPERIAL* Hybrid Tea (Photo on page 29)	Dark crimson	M	AARS 1953. Classic, velvety dark red with shapely buds, full flowers, and rich fragrance. Free flowering, bushy plants have dark green, rather dull foliage. A standard of comparison among reds.
CRIMSON GLORY* Hybrid Tea	Dark crimson	L	Until 'Chrysler Imperial' arrived, this was THE red rose: lovely buds and full, velvety flowers with powerful fragrance. Low, vigorous, spreading plants. Not best in cool climates.
EUROPEANA Floribunda (Photo on page 29)	Ruby red	L	AARS 1968. Low, spreading, strong growing bushes produce very large clusters of bright but deep red blooms. Individual flowers are up to 3 inches across, full and rosette shaped.
EYE PAINT Floribunda (Photo on page 30)	Scarlet	M	Each flower consists of five brilliant scarlet petals, and each bloom is centered by a white eye and tuft of golden stamens. Flowers come in clusters on a vigorous, arching, spreading bush with good glossy foliage. More of a shrub rose than a floribunda.
FLAMING PEACE Hybrid Tea	Red-gold bicolor	M	A color sport of 'Peace', with similar plant and foliage, but a dramatic color departure. As blooms open, petals are blood red inside with gold reverses; mature flowers are purple red and buff.
FORTY-NINER Hybrid Tea	Red-yellow bicolor	M	AARS 1949. A distinct bicolor, the outside of the petals is creamy yellow while the inside is a bright Chinese red that blues somewhat as it ages. Shapely buds on a compact, upright bush.
FRENSHAM Floribunda (Photo on page 30)	Dark crimson	T	Velvety red buds of best hybrid tea form open to semi-double unfading blooms with showy golden stamens. Tall, vigorous, vase-shaped, thorny bushes are excellent hedges or background plants.
GARNETTE Floribunda	Dark crimson	L	A familiar florist rose, the very double, rosette-shaped blooms last seven to ten days indoors. Open flowers never lose their attractiveness. Hollylike foliage is susceptible to mildew.
GRAND MASTERPIECE Hybrid Tea	Bright red	T	Embodies classic red rose qualities. Long, pointed buds spiral open to full blossoms of bright, rich, unfading red on long cutting stems. Plant is tall and especially vigorous.
GYPSY Hybrid Tea	Orange red	T	AARS 1973. Flashing ember red flowers and nearly black red buds are flaunted on vigorous, medium-tall bushes. The healthy foliage is dark bronzy green.
INTERAMA Floribunda	Bright red	M	Brilliant color—and plenty of it—comes from clustered flowers that resemble small hybrid teas. Bushy, free-branching plants have dark green, disease-resistant foliage.

(Continued on next page)

* Also available as a climber.

NAME & TYPE	COLOR	HEIGHT	DESCRIPTION
JENNIFER HART Hybrid Tea	Deep red	M	Pointed, ovoid buds atop long cutting stems open to velvety dark red blossoms full of petals. Plants are vigorous, of medium height or taller, with healthy, semi-glossy foliage.
JOHN S. ARMSTRONG Grandiflora	Dark red	T	AARS 1962. A dark, vibrant red that refuses to turn blue as it ages. Fairly short black red buds open to many-petaled medium-size flowers, singly or in clusters, that last many days cut or on the bush.
KARL HERBST Hybrid Tea	Dark scarlet	M	Sometimes called the "red Peace" because its husky plant and full flowers are reminiscent of its parent. The dark scarlet petals are lighter on the outside, and blooms open best in dry, warm weather.
KENTUCKY DERBY Hybrid Tea	Dark red	T	Very vigorous, upright plants produce a profusion of rich, dark red, pointed to urn-shaped buds. These open to high-centered blooms of 40-50 petals.
LOVE Grandiflora (Photo on page 1)	Red and white	M	AARS 1980. Beautifully pointed buds composed of brilliant red petals with silvery white backs; unfolding flowers are a combination of red and white, while the fully opened, medium-size bloom is completely red. A vigorous, somewhat spreading plant.
MIRANDY Hybrid Tea	Dark red	M	AARS 1945. Outstanding in warm, humid regions, but blooms tend to ball and turn purple where it's cool and foggy. Intensely fragrant, well formed, full flowers; very bushy plant.
MR. LINCOLN Hybrid Tea (Photo on page 28)	Rich red	T	AARS 1965. A completely satisfactory red for all regions: lovely long buds and full, fragrant, open flowers. An easy growing, tall plant with long stems and dark glossy foliage.
NOCTURNE Hybrid Tea	Dark red	M	AARS 1948. Better in the Midwest, East, and South where summers are humid and warm. Longer slimmer buds and not so full a flower as its sister 'Mirandy'. Husky, bushy plant.
OKLAHOMA* Hybrid Tea	Black red	T	The blackest buds imaginable open to very large, rather globular, dusky red blooms that still are beautiful when fully open. Heavy fragrance, lusty grower. Not at its best in cool, foggy areas.
OLD SMOOTHIE Hybrid Tea	Rich red	T	Remarkable in that it is nearly thornless: some stems have no thorns, while others have just a few. Large, rich red, high-centered blooms come on vigorous, upright plants.
OLÉ* Grandiflora (Photo on page 28)	Orange red	M	An individual flower could be mistaken for a tuberous begonia or a carnation. Very double, ruffled and frilled blooms are a blinding red orange. Bushy plants with hollylike leaves.
OLYMPIAD Hybrid Tea (Photo on page 27)	Bright red	T	AARS 1984. Upright plant produces brilliant, nonbluing blossoms on florist-length cutting stems. Long buds spiral open to large, long-lasting flowers with light fragrance. Healthy, dark foliage.
PAPA MEILLAND Hybrid Tea	Dark red	M	Elegance in dark velvety crimson. Long, pointed buds open slowly to very fragrant double blooms even in cool, damp weather—though foliage may mildew then. Upright plant.
PRECIOUS PLATINUM Hybrid Tea	Rich red	M	Practically a foolproof rose, this healthy, husky bush with glossy, disease-resistant foliage bears quantities of fragrant, unfading, rich crimson blooms of medium size.
PROUD LAND Hybrid Tea	Bright red	M	Heavy, penetrating fragrance emanates from the full-petaled, velvety blossoms. Buds are long, pointed, and freely produced on long stems. Vigorous, upright plant.
RAZZLE DAZZLE Floribunda	Red and white	M	Snappy combination of red petals with white on the back inspired the name of this rose. Flower form is classic hybrid tea, with pointed buds and scrolled petal edges.

NAME & TYPE	COLOR	HEIGHT	DESCRIPTION
RED DEVIL Hybrid Tea (Photo on page 30)	Bright, light red	M	Flame red petals have a lighter, almost silvery reverse. Long, lovely buds on long stems open to full, symmetrical flowers that hold their color. Handsome glossy foliage, upright plant.
RED MASTERPIECE Hybrid Tea	Dark red	T	Where days are warm and sunny this red will put on its best performance: full pointed buds opening to velvety blooms that take on black shadings as they open. Rich fragrance, strong plant.
RED RADIANCE* Hybrid Tea	Cerise	T	A standard of dependability among light red roses for over half a century. Flowers have an old-fashioned look—globular buds and cupped, very double blooms. Very vigorous and trouble free.
SARABANDE Floribunda (Photo on page 30)	Oriental red	L	AARS 1960. Flowers are especially brilliant and have clusters of decorative stamens in their centers. Spreading plants, almost always in bloom; ideal for borders or foreground plantings.
SCARLET KNIGHT Grandiflora (Photo on page 30)	Velvety scarlet	M	AARS 1968. Plump black red buds in small clusters unfurl to bright velvety red, thick-petaled blooms about 5 inches across. Bushy, thorny, and vigorous, with dark bronze green leaves.
SHOWBIZ Floribunda (Photo on page 29)	Scarlet	M	AARS 1985. A first-rate landscape shrub offering nearly continuous bloom on a robust, almost disease-proof plant. Long-lasting, semi-double flowers are intense scarlet; petals are ruffled.
SNOWFIRE Hybrid Tea (Photo on page 28)	Red-white bicolor	M	The name describes the colors: brilliant, velvety red with white petal backs. Upright, thorny plants bear handsome, glossy, dark green leaves.
TRUMPETER Floribunda	Orange red	M	Intense, blazing color between orange and red characterizes full, waxy-petaled blossoms; flowers, large for a floribunda, come singly or in small clusters. Glossy foliage resists disease.
VIVA Floribunda	Clear red	M	Between floribunda and hybrid tea in size and habit. Shapely 3-inch flowers come on cutting-length stems from few-flowered clusters. Husky, medium-tall plant.

PINK ROSES

NAME & TYPE	COLOR	HEIGHT	DESCRIPTION
ALMONDEEN Hybrid Tea	Pink and cream blend	M	Delicate warm pink color comes from an overlay of rose pink on honey beige petals. Ovoid buds spiral open to full flowers—singly or in small clusters—on long stems.
ANTIGUA Hybrid Tea	Pink-apricot-gold blend	T	The luscious colors combined in this flower could also qualify it for the multicolor category. Large, shapely blossoms of pink, apricot, and gold come on tall, vigorous plants.
AQUARIUS Grandiflora (Photo on page 35)	Deep rose	T	AARS 1971. The cool rose pink petals are overlaid deeper pink toward the margins. Long, beautifully tapered buds are produced in quantity. Very vigorous, slender bushes.
BETTY PRIOR Floribunda	Shrimp pink	T	All the charm of wild roses and much of the vigor, too. Red buds open to single, shell pink blooms that resemble dogwoods in size and shape. Strong growing, spreading bush with lots of bloom.

* Also available as a climber.

(Continued on next page)

NAME & TYPE	COLOR	HEIGHT	DESCRIPTION
BEWITCHED Hybrid Tea (Photo on page 35)	Rose pink	T	AARS 1967. Stylish, long pointed buds with lighter reverse open slowly to fragrant, "show rose"-type flowers on long, strong stems. Healthy, gray green foliage clothes the vigorous, compact plants.
CAMELOT Grandiflora (Photo on page 36)	Coral pink	T	AARS 1965. The 5-inch, cup-shaped flowers open from rounded buds that nearly always come in clusters. Productivity and general health are its strong points; vigorous with large, dark foliage.
CECILE BRUNNER* Polyantha (Photo on page 20)	Light pink	M	The bush will grow to medium size, but it takes time. Perfect miniature replicas of hybrid tea flowers come continuously throughout the year in graceful, thin-stemmed clusters.
CENTURY TWO Hybrid Tea	Dark rose	M	This has the "ideal" rose buds: large, long, full-petaled, and fragrant. The outside of the petals is slightly deeper in color than the face. Husky plants are upright, bushy, with healthy foliage.
CHARLOTTE ARMSTRONG* Hybrid Tea (Photo on page 36)	Deep red pink	T	AARS 1941. The parent of countless stylish roses produced since its introduction. Famous for its long, elegantly slim buds that open to large, full flowers. Strong, bushy plant.
CHERISH Floribunda	Coral pink	M	AARS 1980. A floribunda in growth and bloom habit, but individual flowers are of hybrid tea size and form. Free-flowering, compact, and rather spreading, with glossy dark foliage.
CHINA DOLL* Polyantha	Rose pink	L	Very double, 1 to 2-inch flowers in rounded clusters can be produced so profusely as to nearly obscure the glossy foliage. Plants grow no more than 1½ feet high and are nearly thornless.
COLOR MAGIC Hybrid Tea	Pink blend	T	AARS 1978. The magic is in the change of colors: creamy pink buds open to ivory centered flowers, then the petals pick up increasing infusions of deep pink. Very vigorous.
CONFIDENCE Hybrid Tea	Pink and cream blend	M	A large, full flower that needs warm weather to open properly. Well-formed buds and open blooms combine pastel shades of pink, peach, and yellow with a distinct fragrance. Upright and bushy.
DAINTY BESS* Hybrid Tea (Photo on page 55)	Rose pink	M	Graceful, perfect, 5-petaled single blossoms are a delicate pink with contrasting maroon red anthers in the flowers' centers. Most of the 3 to 4-inch blooms come in clusters on the upright bushes.
DUET Hybrid Tea (Photo on page 38)	Dusky pink	M	AARS 1961. A terrific flower-producer with a cast-iron constitution. Medium-size buds and blooms are a two-tone dusky pink, darker on the outside of petals, and very long lasting.
EIFFEL TOWER Hybrid Tea	Light pink	T	This rose is as monumental as its name: very long buds, long stems, and one of the tallest plants in the garden. Its pale, cool pink color has an undertone of lavender. Nearly thornless.
ELECTRON Hybrid Tea (Photo on page 38)	Deep rose	M	AARS 1973. Full, glowing rose pink blossoms slowly unfold from pointed buds; the regularly formed open flowers retain their attractiveness. Bushy plant with dark green foliage.
FASHION Floribunda	Coral	L	AARS 1950. The first of the coral-colored floribundas and still an exquisite flower. Ovoid buds in small clusters open to rather cupped 3-inch blooms. Bushy, spreading plant has bronzy foliage.
FIRST LOVE Hybrid Tea (Photo on page 38)	Pearly pink	T	It would be hard to imagine a rose with a longer, more slender and graceful bud. In addition, the plant itself is tall and slender with elongated leaflets. Free blooming and a favorite for cutting.
FIRST PRIZE* Hybrid Tea (Photo on page 37)	Rich pink	L	AARS 1970. Fabulous, very long, spiral buds of a deep pink unfold to really large flowers that are distinctly lighter in the center. Vigorous, spreading bushes are somewhat susceptible to mildew.

* Also available as a climber.

(Continued on page 39)

Tiffany

Pink Roses
modest blush to assertive raspberry

Bewitched

Aquarius

Perfume Delight

...Pink Roses

Rosenelfe

Touch of Class

Rosenelfe

Camelot *Charlotte Armstrong*

First Prize

Royal Highness

Queen Elizabeth

Miss All-American Beauty

...Pink Roses

First Love

Electron

Seashell

Duet

. . . Pink Roses (cont'd.)

NAME & TYPE	COLOR	HEIGHT	DESCRIPTION
FRIENDSHIP Hybrid Tea	Salmon pink	T	AARS 1979. Color will vary from pink through coral and salmon shades, but the blossoms are always long-budded and shapely, carried on good cutting stems. Strong upright bush.
GENE BOERNER Floribunda	Rose pink	M	AARS 1969. In every detail, the buds and flowers are perfect scaled-down models of the best hybrid teas. The clear, rose pink blooms come both singly and in clusters on strong, upright bushes.
HELEN TRAUBEL Hybrid Tea	Salmon	T	AARS 1952. Big, billowing bushes take up more space than many other roses but are well worth it. Great quantities of long pointed buds open quickly to large, rather loose flowers on flexible stems.
JADIS Hybrid Tea	Rose pink	T	Powerful fragrance and beautiful form are noteworthy. Slender, urn-shaped buds produce moderately full flowers of pure bright pink on a tall and slender bush. A profuse bloomer.
MICHELE MEILLAND Hybrid Tea	Creamy pink	M	Produces only medium-size flowers, but the rate of production is rapid and nearly each bloom is perfect. Color varies from creamy pink to creamy amber. Vigorous, bushy plant.
MILESTONE Hybrid Tea	Coral pink	T	In chameleon style, ovoid rose red buds open to full coral pink flowers with light centers; color slowly darkens to coral red before petals fall.
MISS ALL-AMERICAN BEAUTY Hybrid Tea (Photo on page 37)	Cerise	M	AARS 1968. A big, bold blossom in a color you can't miss: something between a deep "shocking" pink and light red. Ovoid buds and well formed open flowers come on leathery-leaved, very husky plants.
MON CHERI Hybrid Tea	Pink to red	M	AARS 1982. A chameleon of roses: soft pink buds open out and become velvety red wherever sun strikes the petals.
PEGGY LEE Hybrid Tea	Light pink	M	This sport of 'Century Two' features all the virtues of that rose with a different coloring—delicate light pink. Elegant buds and large blossoms exude a sweet fragrance.
PERFUME DELIGHT Hybrid Tea (Photo on page 35)	Deep pink	M	AARS 1974. Rich, spicy fragrance is one asset, another is the flawless, long, spiraled bud that unfurls to perfect, satiny pink, 5-inch blossoms. Plants are upright and compact.
PICTURE* Hybrid Tea	Pink and salmon blend	L	A time-honored favorite bearing "picture perfect" buds and blooms in several profuse bursts throughout the flowering season. The medium-size flowers are reminiscent of pink camellias. Bushy.
PINK FAVORITE Hybrid Tea	Rose pink	M	This variety boasts some of the most beautiful foliage known among roses: shiny green, large, and leathery. Large, well-formed buds open quickly. Very vigorous, healthy.
PINK PARFAIT Grandiflora	Creamy pink	M	AARS 1961. Difficult to classify. The perfectly formed buds are floribunda size, and blooms come in floribunda profusion; but the bush is too large for that class, yet it is shorter than most grandifloras. A healthy, vigorous plant, and a delightful cut-flower rose.
PINK PEACE Hybrid Tea	Deep rose	T	Not really a pink duplicate of 'Peace', yet it is a large, full and shapely, intense deep pink with heavy fragrance. Free-flowering, very vigorous and upright bushes, but especially prone to rust.
PRISTINE Hybrid Tea	Blush	M	Not white, but just barely pink, the delicate color is displayed against glossy dark green leaves. Heavy-substanced flowers of 30-35 petals open well in all weather from lovely urn-shaped buds.
PROMISE Hybrid Tea	Light pink	T	Clear, light pink color holds from ovoid bud through open flower: large blossoms can have as many as 45 petals. Foliage is light green and glossy.

* Also available as a climber.

(Continued on next page)

NAME & TYPE	COLOR	HEIGHT	DESCRIPTION
QUEEN ELIZABETH* Grandiflora (Photo on page 37)	Clear pink	T	AARS 1955. For all practical purposes, a shrub rose—suitable for hedges and background plantings. Radiant pink, medium-size blooms develop from compact, pointed buds in small clusters. Extremely vigorous, tall, bulky bushes.
RADIANCE* Hybrid Tea	Rose pink	T	An old-fashioned-looking rose that for over half a century has been the example for good performance, even when neglected. Ovoid buds open to double, cupped, two-toned blooms. Rugged bush.
ROSE GAUJARD Hybrid Tea	Raspberry-white bicolor	T	A beautiful bicolor of white and raspberry rose, the white base color is brushed with pink to leave only the centers and bases of petals white. Very shapely, large blooms on an easy-to-grow bush.
ROSENELFE Floribunda (Photo on page 36)	Rose pink	M	Perfect, regular, camellialike blooms of pure pink are carried in small clusters, each flower about 3 inches across. Healthy, vigorous plants are upright with attractive dark green foliage.
ROSE PARADE Floribunda	Peach pink	M	AARS 1975. Bushy, spreading plants clothed in disease-resistant, dark green foliage produce quantities of perfectly formed, small buds and full, 3-inch blooms.
ROYAL HIGHNESS Hybrid Tea (Photo on page 37)	Blush pink	T	AARS 1963. Porcelainlike blush pink buds and flowers are of the highest quality. Long pointed buds, one to a stem, slowly unfold to magnificent, full, open blooms. Upright bushes.
SEA PEARL Floribunda	Pink and cream blend	T	Long and shapely buds combine peach to salmon tones with creamy yellow, depth of color varying according to weather. A good cut flower on vigorous plants with bronze new growth.
SEASHELL Hybrid Tea (Photo on page 38)	Salmon	M	AARS 1976. Color can vary from peach to light orange. Deep apricot buds unfold into rich, yellow-tinted, full and fragrant blossoms. Good dark green foliage on an upright, profuse bush.
SIMPLICITY Floribunda	Bright pink	M	This lavishly flowering shrub just happens to be a rose! Vigor, freedom of bloom, and abundant disease-proof foliage make 'Simplicity' ideal for hedges and mass plantings.
SONIA Grandiflora	Coral	M	Noted for medium-small but perfectly formed buds and long-lasting, high-centered open flowers. Color varies, according to weather, from soft to deep coral; vigorous, with plenty of deep green foliage.
SOUTH SEAS Hybrid Tea	Coral salmon	T	Really large but gracefully ruffled open flowers develop from slow-opening buds of a deep shell pink. Notably vigorous, slightly spreading bushes have bronze-tinted foliage.
SUNRISE-SUNSET Hybrid Tea	Pink and cream blend	M	A distinctive mingling of soft pink and cream, sometimes with tinges of tannish lavender at the base of petals. Attractive long buds open to blossoms with light centers.
SUNSET JUBILEE Hybrid Tea	Pink and yellow blend	M	In cool weather it's pink and nearly white, but when weather warms so do the colors—to light yellow and coppery pink. Long buds slowly unfurl to full flowers that hold an attractive shape.
SWARTHMORE Hybrid Tea	Cherry pink	T	Fabulously long buds of cherry red with darker margins unfold into very long-lasting open flowers of a lighter pink but still with the darker edge. Free-flowering, upright bush.
SWEET SURRENDER Hybrid Tea	Silvery pink	T	AARS 1983. Heady fragrance is one of this rose's outstanding characteristics. Upright plant with leathery foliage produces long stems that carry many-petaled, high-centered cool pink blooms.
THE FAIRY Polyantha (Photo on page 13)	Pale pink	L	The individual flowers are unimportant, but the numbers of them per cluster creates the effect. Bushes are low, spreading, very vigorous, with fernlike, disease-proof foliage.

NAME & TYPE	COLOR	HEIGHT	DESCRIPTION
TIFFANY* Hybrid Tea (Photo on page 35)	Warm pink	T	AARS 1955. The large and long buds have the perfection of a finely cut jewel, and they open to lush, double, intensely fragrant blooms. At its best out of cool, damp regions. Upright.
TOUCH OF CLASS Hybrid Tea (Photo on page 36)	Coral pink	M	AARS 1986. Heavy-petaled, long-lasting blossoms shade from coral into a vibrant warm pink. Large, moderately full flowers open from spiraled, tapered buds. Foliage is large and glossy.
TRIBUTE Hybrid Tea	Dark pink	T	Glowing color, as though lighted from within, helps make 'Tribute' a standout. Long, tapered buds and large, open blossoms of vivid cherry pink come steadily throughout the season. Foliage is glossy and dark.
VOGUE Floribunda	Cherry coral	M	AARS 1952. Slender, stylish buds suggested this rose be named after the *Vogue* models of similar style. Upright, bushy plants bearing medium-size clusters of very fragrant flowers.

ORANGE ROSES

NAME & TYPE	COLOR	HEIGHT	DESCRIPTION
APRICOT NECTAR Floribunda	Creamy apricot	M	AARS 1966. Large flower clusters are loaded with luscious creamy apricot hybrid tealike blooms, each of which may be up to 4 inches across. Healthy, vigorous, and prolific bushes.
ARIZONA Grandiflora	Copper orange	T	AARS 1975. Here's a candidate for specimen shrub or tall hedge planting. Urn-shaped buds open to flowers of glowing, gold-tinted orange shades, highlighted against copper-tinted, dark, leathery foliage.
BAHIA Floribunda (Photo on page 43)	Pink orange	M	AARS 1974. Full, vivid orange blooms with coral and yellow tints come in small clusters on bushy, upright plants. Flowers are very double and fragrant.
BING CROSBY Hybrid Tea	Mandarin orange	M	AARS 1981. "Persimmon" is the nearly unanimous description of this rose's glowing orange color. Medium length buds open into full-petaled, lightly fragrant blossoms. Vigorous, with good foliage.
BRANDY Hybrid Tea	Buff orange	M	AARS 1982. Glowing golden apricot blooms, opening from burnt orange buds, suggested the name. Large, broad-petaled flowers open well in all weather. Red bronze new foliage completes the color scheme.
COMMAND PERFORMANCE Hybrid Tea	Orange scarlet	T	AARS 1971. An offspring of 'Tropicana' of similar glowing orange color. As the long buds unfold, petal edges roll back to give blooms a star effect. Vigorous, but mildew prone.
DIAMOND JUBILEE Hybrid Tea	Buff orange	M	AARS 1948. Light buff orange blooms open slowly and are at their best when half or more open; in poor weather the buds are not always attractive. Very fragrant, strong and upright.
FIRST EDITION Floribunda (Photo on page 43)	Coral orange	L	AARS 1977. The perfection of hybrid tea form brought down to floribunda size, coming both singly and in clusters. Plant is low but quite spreading, with bright green, leathery leaves.
FOLKLORE Hybrid Tea	Soft orange	T	Large, long, shapely buds open to orange flowers softened by a pink overcast; petal backs are a harmonizing creamy gold. Bush is tall and extremely vigorous, with handsome, glossy foliage.

* Also available as a climber.

(Continued on next page)

NAME & TYPE	COLOR	HEIGHT	DESCRIPTION
FRAGRANT CLOUD Hybrid Tea (Photo on page 43)	Coral orange	M	Long scarlet orange buds unfold to coral orange, 30-petaled blooms that exude a delightfully intense fragrance; some come singly, others in small clusters. Bush is husky and trouble-free.
GINGERSNAP Floribunda	Mandarin orange	M	Nearly hybrid-tea-size flowers of glowing orange come in clusters on a compact plant bearing deep bronze purple new growth.
IMPATIENT Floribunda	Orange red	T	AARS 1984. Vivid orange scarlet buds, freely produced on upright plant, open to 3-inch blossoms of a softer shade. New growth is mahogany colored, maturing to dark, glossy green.
MARGO KOSTER* Polyantha (Photo on page 20)	Light orange	L	Almost round buds are composed of many shell-like petals that open into small cupped flowers resembling ranunculus. Color is soft coral orange. Large bloom clusters on a twiggy, compact bush.
MARINA Floribunda	Coral orange	M	AARS 1981. Dark, glossy green foliage on an upright plant makes handsome contrast with the vibrant orange flowers. Shapely buds come both in clusters and one to a stem.
MEDALLION Hybrid Tea (Photo on page 44)	Light buff orange	T	AARS 1973. Everything about this rose is large, from the extra long buds to the open flowers, even to the plant. Buff apricot in bud, the open flowers have pink tones. Upright.
MISS LIBERTÉ Hybrid Tea	Dark orange	M	Highly polished leaves form a striking backdrop for full, coral orange flowers. Buds are deep orange, blossoms take on shades of red as they mature. Husky plant is somewhat spreading.
MOJAVE Hybrid Tea (Photo on page 43)	Burnt orange	T	AARS 1954. Stylish burnt orange buds, veined a darker shade, open to 25-petaled light apricot orange blooms. Vigorous, very slender bushes have dark canes and glossy dark green leaves.
MONTEZUMA Hybrid Tea (Photo on page 44)	Coral orange	T	Beautifully formed nearly red buds lighten as they open to coral salmon (or orange coral in warm weather). Robust plants are slightly spreading with leaves that start out bronzy red.
OLDTIMER Hybrid Tea	Bronze apricot	T	Very large blooms develop from long, streamlined buds—all petals having an elegant satin texture. Color is golden apricot with tints of bronze or copper. Leathery, pointed leaves; upright bush.
PROMINENT Grandiflora (Photo on page 44)	Brilliant orange	M	AARS 1977. A neon brightness to the pure deep orange color makes this rose impossible to overlook. Petals recurve so that each forms a point, creating a starlike flower. The long-lasting blooms are displayed against thick, glossy foliage.
SHREVEPORT Grandiflora	Salmon orange	T	AARS 1982. Artful blending of orange, salmon, coral, and yellow gives overall impression of soft orange. Shapely buds and 4-inch blooms come one to a stem on strong-growing plants.
SPARTAN Floribunda	Salmon orange	M	Blooms are a little larger than the average floribunda. Burnt orange, well-formed buds open to very full coral orange flowers that have an old-fashioned look. Vigorous and upright bushes.
SUNDOWNER Grandiflora	Pure orange	T	AARS 1979. Exuberantly vigorous tall bushes produce their glowing, 40-petaled flowers in small clusters during summer, but one bud per stem during the spring bloom season.
SUNFIRE Floribunda	Mandarin orange	M	Vibrant 'Tropicana' orange color is displayed in 3-inch hybrid-tealike flowers that come in clusters but on stems long enough for cutting individually. Medium-tall plants have abundant foliage.
TROPICANA* Hybrid Tea (Photo on page 44)	Orange salmon	T	AARS 1963. Forerunner of the fluorescent, orange colors. Medium size, pointed buds produce full, rather cupped open flowers, singly or in clusters. Vigorous, semispreading, and mildew-prone.

*Also available as a climber.

Fragrant Cloud   *Mojave*

Orange Roses

buff, apricot, bronze, & neon orange

Bahia   *First Edition*

Montezuma   *Tropicana*

Medallion

…Orange Roses

Prominent

Sutter's Gold

Cathedral

Marmalade

Multicolor Roses

**warm-toned rainbows,
soft or bright**

Charisma

...Multicolor Roses

Redgold

Peace

Granada   *Chicago Peace*

MULTICOLOR ROSES

NAME & TYPE	COLOR	HEIGHT	DESCRIPTION
BROADWAY Hybrid Tea	Pink and yellow blend	T	AARS 1986. Urn-shaped golden buds are suffused with pink; as the flowers open, the pink tones increase and intensify at the edges of the petals. A strong, upright bush characterized by dark, leathery leaves.
CARIBIA * **(Harry Wheatcroft)** Hybrid Tea	Red and yellow	L	The jester of the rose garden, 'Caribia' has bright yellow petals irregularly streaked with brilliant red. Bronzy foliage complements the color scheme.
CATHEDRAL Floribunda (Photo on page 45)	Orange apricot	L	AARS 1976. Small clusters of well-formed buds open to salmon-tinted, ruffled blossoms—each stem a perfect bouquet. Glossy, copper-tinted foliage densely covers compact, bushy plants.
CHARISMA Floribunda (Photo on page 45)	Yellow, orange, and red blend	M	AARS 1978. Rounded, spreading plants flaunt very double, rosette-shaped small blooms of brilliant golden yellow, edged orange red; the red color predominates as the flowers age.
CHERRY-VANILLA Hybrid Tea	Yellow and pink blend	T	An engaging, changeable blend of cream to yellow petals infused with varying amounts of reddish pink from the petal edges. Plants are tall and upright.
CHICAGO PEACE Hybrid Tea (Photo on page 46)	Pink and copper blend	M	A color sport of 'Peace' in which all the virtues of foliage, plant, and magnificent flower form have been retained but in a more lively flower—bronzy yellow, deep pink, and copper.
CIRCUS Floribunda	Yellow and red blend	L	AARS 1956. Yellow buds in the best hybrid tea style are blended with red at the edges; as blooms open, more red infuses the petals to give buff and pink shadings. Glossy foliage; spreading.
CIRCUS PARADE Floribunda	Orange, buff, and pink blend	M	A color sport of the floribunda 'Circus' in which the colors have intensified to a buff yellow with more pink and red in the open flower. Plants are bushy and compact, but larger than 'Circus', and have larger leaves.
DOUBLE DELIGHT * Hybrid Tea (Photo on front cover)	Red, cream, and white blend	M	AARS 1977. Unmistakable blooms of camellialike form: creamy white with cherry red brushed on petal edges. The amount of red varies according to weather and increases as the flower ages. Easy-to-grow, spreading bush with glossy leaves.
FASCINATION Hybrid Tea	Ivory, apricot, coral, and gold blend	M	Artful combination of ivory, apricot, coral, and gold appears in full, large flowers that mimic peonies in size and form. Husky bush grows easily and has many canes.
GARDEN PARTY Hybrid Tea	Ivory and pink blend	M	AARS 1960. Finely crafted long ivory buds are tinted pink on the petal margins and this intensifies as they open to beautiful, stiffly perfect blooms. Vigorous, upright; sometimes mildews.
GRANADA Grandiflora (Photo on page 46)	Red and yellow blend	M	AARS 1964. Nasturtium red, light yellow, and pink blend together into notably fragrant and very long-lasting flowers. Well-formed slender buds often come in clusters. Hollylike, dark foliage.
LAS VEGAS Hybrid Tea	Orange-yellow bicolor	M	Brilliant color is this rose's trademark. Shapely, pointed buds yield medium-size flowers that are vibrant red orange; the backs of the petals are golden yellow blending to orange. The blossoms open quickly.
LITTLE DARLING Floribunda	Pink and cream blend	T	Darling, but not little. Long, arching canes make this more of a shrub than a typical floribunda. Each pink and cream flower is perfectly formed and long lasting. Vigorous, trouble free.

(Continued on next page)

NAME & TYPE	COLOR	HEIGHT	DESCRIPTION
MARMALADE Hybrid Tea (Photo on page 45)	Orange and gold bicolor	T	Bicolored blooms display marmalade orange petals that show gold undersides, the two colors combining in elegantly tapered buds. Fragrant, medium-size blossoms are backed by bright green leaves.
MATADOR Floribunda	Scarlet and yellow bicolor	M	As flashy as its namesake, in colors that would stimulate the laziest of bulls. Short pointed buds open to long-lasting bicolor blossoms: orange red on petal faces, yellow on the backs.
PEACE* Hybrid Tea (Photo on page 46)	Yellow and pink blend	M	AARS 1946. Full, ovoid buds are yellow touched with pink or red; they gradually unfold to yellow petals widely edged pink. A glorious half to fully open bloom. Strong, spreading bush.
REDGOLD Floribunda (Photo on page 46)	Gold and red blend	L	AARS 1971. Golden yellow buds edged in red become less yellow as flowers open and the red suffuses more of the blooms. Nicely shaped buds on a compact, bushy, well-foliaged plant.
SUTTER'S GOLD* Hybrid Tea (Photo on page 45)	Yellow and orange blend	T	AARS 1950. Powerfully fragrant, blended yellow, with elegant long buds. Most attractive in cool climates where its flowers open more slowly and hold color better. Strong, willowy bush.
TALISMAN* Hybrid Tea	Yellow, orange, and copper blend	M	A favorite bicolor for nearly half a century. Flat-topped buds are golden on the outside, copper orange inside, and open to cream and pink blooms. Bright green foliage, upright bush.
VOODOO Hybrid Tea	Orange, yellow, and pink blend	T	AARS 1986. Yellow orange buds open to large flowers that soften to yellow peach shades and fade to pink. Tall, upright bush carries plenty of glossy, dark bronze green foliage.
YANKEE DOODLE Hybrid Tea	Yellow and apricot blend	T	AARS 1976. Big, full-petaled flowers are a bicolor blend: the glowing orange salmon petals are backed with yellow. Very vigorous, upright, and bushy, with glossy, dark foliage.

YELLOW ROSES

NAME & TYPE	COLOR	HEIGHT	DESCRIPTION
ARLENE FRANCIS Hybrid Tea	Golden yellow	M	A notably fragrant, clear golden yellow. Beautifully formed, long pointed buds develop into moderately double, large blooms. Bushes are somewhat spreading, mantled in glossy, dark green leaves.
ECLIPSE Hybrid Tea (Photo on page 50)	Medium yellow	M	An old favorite, loved for its long, stylish buds. Open flowers are not especially lovely, but bud production is plentiful on a very vigorous, upright bush with grayed green leaves.
GOLD BADGE Floribunda	Golden yellow	L	Brilliant, unfading flowers are large and in small sprays, similar to small hybrid tea. Glossy dark green foliage clothes a fairly low, spreading bush.
GOLDEN MASTERPIECE Hybrid Tea	Deep yellow	M	Long, large buds expand into one of the largest blooms among roses; the rich color holds well. Foliage is glossy on an upright plant.
GOLD MEDAL Grandiflora	Deep gold	T	Great vigor and good health are the winning traits of this rose. Long, ovoid golden yellow buds (sometimes tinged with pink) spiral open to large, full-petaled blossoms in small clusters.
IRISH GOLD Hybrid Tea (Photo on page 50)	Light yellow	M	Flawless, full but pointed buds of pale yellow gradually unfurl to very double blooms tinged with pink in cool weather; petals become pointed at tips as edges recurve. Bright green foliage.

* Also available as a climber.

NAME & TYPE	COLOR	HEIGHT	DESCRIPTION
KATHERINE LOKER Floribunda	Butter yellow	M	Clear yellow hybrid-tealike blossoms come singly as well as in small clusters. Free-flowering plant features abundant semi-glossy foliage.
KING'S RANSOM Hybrid Tea (Photo on page 50)	Deep yellow	M	AARS 1962. Classically formed long buds open symmetrically into unfading chrome yellow, 6-inch flowers. Vigorous, easy-to-grow plants adorned with dark, glossy leaves.
LOWELL THOMAS Hybrid Tea	Deep yellow	M	AARS 1944. For many years the standard bright, medium-yellow rose with the ability to perform well in all regions. Long pointed buds, 5-inch double blooms, and an erect, compact bush.
NEW DAY Hybrid Tea	Soft yellow	M	Classic, shapely buds and clear color are features of this 30-petaled, fragrant rose. Upright, thorny plants carry leathery, gray green foliage.
OREGOLD Hybrid Tea (Photo on page 50)	Saffron yellow	M	AARS 1975. A deep, rich color due to the tawny tint in the basic golden yellow. Long, pointed buds develop into full and shapely, softer yellow blossoms. Vigorous, bushy, with good dark foliage.
SUMMER SUNSHINE Hybrid Tea (Photo on page 50)	Pure bright yellow	M	The most brilliant pure yellow imaginable, both in bud and open bloom. Beautifully chiseled buds are complemented by shiny green, bronze-tinted foliage. Plants are upright and bushy.
SUNBONNET Floribunda	Bright yellow	L	Another good foreground plant with low, bushy growth. Bright, shapely buds and double flowers, singly or in clusters, with the fragrance of licorice. Glossy, dark green foliage.
SUNBRIGHT Hybrid Tea	Deep yellow	T	Robust, fast-growing plant produces a near-continuous display of bright blossoms backed by glossy foliage. Long, urn-shaped buds open to large, moderately double flowers that hold their color.
SUN FLARE Floribunda	Lemon yellow	L	AARS 1983. Low, compact, bushy plants freely produce shapely, fragrant 3-inch blossoms in small to moderate-size clusters; bright lemon color fades little. Dense, glossy, hollylike foliage.
SUNSPRITE Floribunda	Bright yellow	M	This upright, well-foliaged plant is the backdrop for perfectly formed, unfading yellow flowers in small clusters. The bright color is striking; the plant is early-flowering.

WHITE ROSES

NAME & TYPE	COLOR	HEIGHT	DESCRIPTION
EVENING STAR Floribunda	Pure white	M	Not quite a hybrid tea; not a floribunda, either. But its lovely form, good garden performance, and lasting ability as a cut flower make classification unimportant. The medium-size, fragrant flowers come in small clusters set off by dark, healthy foliage.
FRAU KARL DRUSCHKI Hybrid Perpetual	Pure white	T	A classic dating from 1901. Hybrid tea by parentage, but a hybrid perpetual (see page 14) in growth habit. Long, pointed buds sometimes are tinged pink, but always open to sparkling white. In mild regions its canes grow so long it can be used as a climber.
FRENCH LACE Floribunda	Pinkish white	M	AARS 1982. The very full-petaled blooms open to display much of the charm of old-fashioned roses. These large, buff white flowers come on spreading plants with dark green foliage.

(Continued on page 51)

Oregold   *Eclipse*   *Summer Sunshine*

King's Ransom

Yellow Roses
the rose-garden sunbeams

Irish Gold

NAME & TYPE	COLOR	HEIGHT	DESCRIPTION
HONOR Hybrid Tea	Pure white	T	AARS 1980. In all climates, this fast-growing, vigorous plant puts out a plentiful crop of satiny white, well-formed blossoms from pointed buds. Leathery, olive green foliage.
ICEBERG Floribunda (Photo on page 53)	Pure white	T	More of a large shrub than a typical floribunda. Well-formed buds are long and pointed, while open flowers are nearly hybrid tea size. Vigorous plant covered with healthy light green leaves.
IVORY FASHION Floribunda (Photo on page 52)	Ivory	M	AARS 1959. A floribunda of hybrid tea refinement. Attractively pointed long buds open to semi-double, 4-inch blooms with golden stamens in the centers. Long lasting when cut.
JOHN F. KENNEDY Hybrid Tea (Photo on page 52)	Greenish white	T	Impeccably formed, long buds are distinctly tinged green in cool weather, otherwise are pure white with petals spiraling open to a beautifully formed, full bloom. Better in warm regions.
LOUISIANA Hybrid Tea	Ivory white	T	Classic, long, cream white buds come on long cutting stems, open into large, full-petaled blooms; best flower development where nights are warm. Very vigorous plants with leathery foliage.
PASCALI Hybrid Tea (Photo on page 53)	Pure white	T	AARS 1969. More dependable than many other whites for perfectly formed, medium-size buds and flowers in all climates. Abundantly produced on upright bushes with dark foliage.
WHITE LIGHTNIN' Grandiflora	Creamy white	M	AARS 1981. Short plants for a grandiflora, but with the expected vigor. Somewhat ruffled petals give distinct personality to the citrus-scented, creamy white blossoms. Glossy, mildew-resistant foliage.
WHITE MASTERPIECE Hybrid Tea (Photo on page 53)	White	M	Flawless, classic form is the most noteworthy characteristic. Large, ovoid buds open into full blooms with pointed petal tips, the outer petals becoming tinted with yellow. Lush green foliage.

LAVENDER ROSES

NAME & TYPE	COLOR	HEIGHT	DESCRIPTION
ANGEL FACE* Floribunda (Photo on page 52)	Rosy lavender	L	AARS 1969. The deep lavender color is enlivened by rose tints and is beautifully complemented by bronze-tinged deep green foliage. Ruffled, very double, fragrant blooms. Spreading plant.
BLUE GIRL* **(Kolner Karneval)** Hybrid Tea	Silvery lavender	M	Cup-shaped silvery lilac flowers with telling fragrance bloom freely on good cutting stems. Vigorous, rounded bushes are densely covered with dark, glossy foliage.
BLUE NILE Hybrid Tea	Rich lavender	T	Exotic rich lavender blossoms are noted for lovely form and intense fragrance as well as luscious color. Husky, bushy plants are clothed in bronze-tinted dark green foliage.
DEEP PURPLE Floribunda	Plum purple	M	Usual color range of flowers is from magenta to light plum, not purple, despite the name. Plants are very vigorous and have attractive, dark, disease-resistant leaves.
HEIRLOOM Hybrid Tea	Lavender and magenta blend	M	The darkest color of the lavender varieties, this has lilac to purple buds opening to magenta flowers that lighten to lilac as they age. Fragrant, with medium-size, pointed buds.
INTRIGUE Floribunda	Purple red	M	AARS 1984. Globular black purple buds open to attractively formed plum-colored blossoms with intense fragrance; bloom size and small number per cluster suggest a small hybrid tea.

(Continued on page 54)

White & Lavender Roses

regal, elegant, cool, unusual

John F. Kennedy

Angel Face

Paradise

Ivory Fashion

Sterling Silver

Pascali

Iceberg

Lavender Pinocchio

White Masterpiece

NAME & TYPE	COLOR	HEIGHT	DESCRIPTION
LADY X Hybrid Tea	Pink lavender	T	The tallest and huskiest plant of these lavender roses, but the color is the least blue of any of them. Long, elegant, pale lavender pink buds unfurl gracefully to full, double flowers.
LAVENDER PINOCCHIO Floribunda (Photo on page 53)	Lavender blend	M	Lavender, but with definite shadings of brown and saffron yellow—an unmistakable color assortment. Clusters of moderately double flowers are freely produced on a vigorous bush.
PARADISE* Hybrid Tea (Photo on page 52)	Lavender and red blend	M	AARS 1979. Beautifully formed buds and open flowers, a vigorous bush, and an absolutely distinctive color arrangement: silvery lavender petals edged in ruby red, the red tones spreading over more petal surface as the flowers age. Foliage is glossy and deep green.
PATSY CLINE Hybrid Tea	Silver lavender and red	M	A color combination similar to but lighter than 'Paradise'. One parent, 'Double Delight', imparted color pattern, other parent, 'Angel Face', contributed shades of lavender. Flowers are fragrant.
SMOKY Hybrid Tea	Lavender blend	M	The color is nearly impossible to describe because it varies greatly according to weather: purple, smoky plum, raspberry, or even a deep, smoldering burnt orange. A certain conversation piece.
STERLING SILVER Hybrid Tea (Photo on page 53)	Silvery lavender	M	A delicious, "old rose" fragrance emanates from the delicate silvery lavender, ruffled and cup-shaped blossoms. Tends to produce floribundalike clusters. Bush is moderately vigorous; prune lightly.

CLIMBING ROSES

Climbing roses of all kinds are listed here alphabetically by name. Under each name is given the class: climbing hybrid tea (CHT), climbing tea (CT), climbing grandiflora (CGR), climbing floribunda (CF), climbing polyantha (CP), large-flowered climber (LCL), pillar (P). Roses with abbreviation CL (climbing) before their names are climbing sports of bush roses. See pages 86-87 for discussion of the various types. Indications for height reflect length to which canes may grow: short (S) is to 10 feet; medium (M) is 10-18 feet; tall (T) is more than 18 feet.

NAME & TYPE	COLOR	HEIGHT	DESCRIPTION
ALOHA P	Two-tone pink	S	Glossy foliage and restrained growth habit mark this as a good pillar rose or even large shrub. Large, full-petaled flowers are rose pink with darker petal reverses.
AMERICA LCL (Photo on page 58)	Coral pink	S	AARS 1976. Beautiful buds and large, full blooms of the best hybrid tea form adorn these vigorous plants throughout the season. Good grown as a pillar rose.
BLAZE LCL	Bright scarlet	M	Clusters of 2 to 3-inch, double flowers smother the plants over a long spring season, then continue in smaller bursts through summer and fall. Slight fragrance. Tough and trouble-free.
CL CECILE BRUNNER CP (Photo on page 20)	Light pink	T	A vigorous and easy grower, producing an enormous crop of its renowned small hybrid tea-style blossoms in the first flush of spring bloom. Later flowering is less profuse.
CL CHARLOTTE ARMSTRONG CHT (Photo on page 36)	Deep red pink	M	A strong-growing but moderate-size climber. Like the bush, a heavy producer of elegant, pointed buds.

* Also available as a climber.

(Continued on page 56)

Climbing Roses

extending the boundaries of the rose garden

Gloire de Dijon

Climbing Dainty Bess

Joseph's Coat

Paul's Scarlet Climber

NAME & TYPE	COLOR	HEIGHT	DESCRIPTION
CL CHRYSLER IMPERIAL CHT (Photo on page 29)	Dark crimson	T	The heavily fragrant, dusky red blooms that made the bush famous, but on a very vigorous, wide-spreading climber. Foliage may need watching for mildew.
CL CRIMSON GLORY CHT	Deep red	M	Much better than the bush form, primarily because you get so much more plant to produce the intensely fragrant, black-shaded blossoms. Longer stems and somewhat larger flowers are another bonus.
CL DAINTY BESS CHT (Photo on page 55)	Rose pink	S	A restrained but vigorous climber for small spaces or pillar training, it can even be left to grow as a large, fountain-shaped shrub. A continual supplier of 5-petaled blossoms in small clusters.
DON JUAN P	Deep crimson	S	A pillar-climber with 8 to 10-foot canes growing straight up. Deep, velvety red buds of best hybrid tea form and size come singly or in small clusters on long stems, and open well in all climates.
DORTMUND LCL (Photo on page 58)	Cherry red	S	A Kordesii climber (see page 17) that also can be a ground cover or shrub. Beautiful, glossy, hollylike foliage. Three-inch flowers are single, bright cherry red with white centers, in large clusters.
CL ETOILE DE HOLLANDE CHT	Dark crimson	T	In its second half-century now, but still a fine rich red in all climates. Lovely high-centered buds open to heavily fragrant, unfading blooms on long stems. Vigorous.
CL FIRST PRIZE CHT (Photo on page 37)	Rich pink	M	The spring crop of flowers is profuse; scattered bloom during the rest of the year, but those blooms can be crowd-stoppers—even larger and more impressive than those on the bush.
GLOIRE DE DIJON CT (Photo on page 55)	Buff, salmon, and cream blend	T	A climbing tea rose (see page 10) dating from 1853. Differing in flower style from modern roses, but equal to the best newer ones in vigor and flower productivity. Full-petaled blooms combine buff, yellow, and pink shades. Will grow in part shade.
GOLDEN SHOWERS LCL	Daffodil yellow	T	AARS 1957. Introduced as a pillar rose, but can be a full-fledged climber in mild climates. Pointed butter yellow buds and lighter, semi-double open blooms. Very free flowering with excellent foliage.
HANDEL LCL	Cream and pink blend	M	Use it as a climber or a pillar—either way you will get quantities of wavy, semi-double blossoms that open from attractive buds. Color is creamy pink, edged in reddish pink; flowers in small clusters.
HIGH NOON LCL	Golden yellow	M	AARS 1948. Similar in many respects to 'Golden Showers'—a pillar or rampant climber, depending upon climate. Buds are flushed with red, and the entire effect is more golden than pure yellow.
JOSEPH'S COAT LCL (Photo on page 55)	Red, orange, and yellow blend	S	The accent is on versatility: use it as a climber or as a free-standing shrub. Color changes from yellow buds through orange and red shadings to crimson mature blooms in floribundalike clusters.
KASSEL LCL (Photo on page 58)	Coral orange	S	Easily a climber in mild regions, but can be used as a shrub anywhere; canes are long and arching. Flowers of hybrid tea size and shape come in small clusters: scarlet orange buds, coral red blooms.
CL MRS. SAM McGREDY CHT (Photo on page 58)	Copper, red, and salmon blend	T	Flawless, classically tapered buds are copper scarlet with salmon to apricot color on the inside of the petals. New growth is a show in itself—plum bronze, passing to dark green. Very free-flowering.
NEW DAWN LCL	Pale pink	T	The first ever to be patented, and the first really cold-tolerant climbing rose having hybrid tealike blooms. Flowers come in small clusters. Can be used also as a pillar type or bank cover.
PAUL'S SCARLET CLIMBER LCL (Photo on page 55)	Bright red	S	A famous and widely planted cluster-flowering double red with one long and very profuse spring flowering season. Brilliant color is unfading. Vigorous; hardier than hybrid tea climbers.

NAME & TYPE	COLOR	HEIGHT	DESCRIPTION
CL PEACE CHT (Photo on page 46)	Yellow and pink blend	T	Extremely vigorous, so give it plenty of wall or fence space. The same impressive flowers and fine foliage as the bush, but more prolific once the climber is established. Generally more satisfactory than the bush form in the warm-winter Southwest.
PINATA LCL	Yellow and orange	S	Glossy foliage sets off floribunda-style flowers of glowing gold overcast with orange red. Growth is restrained, somewhat shrubby; use it as a small climber or free-standing shrub.
CL QUEEN ELIZABETH CGR (Photo on page 37)	Clear pink	M	Just as vigorous and prolific—indestructible, really—as the widely planted bush form.
RED FOUNTAIN P	Deep red	S	A floribunda-style pillar rose or short climber. Clusters of medium-size, informal flowers are dark and velvety, coming from buds that verge on black.
RHONDA LCL	Coral pink	S	One that can be used as a pillar type, as well as fanned out horizontally for a restrained climber. Globular buds in small clusters open to medium-size blooms.
ROYAL GOLD LCL	Golden yellow	M	Glowing yellow, perfect hybrid tea buds on a natural climber or pillar type—larger in mild regions. Blooms come singly or in small clusters and retain color and form as they open.
ROYAL SUNSET LCL	Orange blend	T	Basically orange buds of the best hybrid tea form and size open to large, fairly double buff apricot blooms that pale to a creamy peach in hot weather. Glossy deep green leaves.
CL SNOWBIRD CHT	Creamy white	M	Has something of the refinement of old tea roses: soft green foliage, slender stems, lovely pointed buds and full, fragrant, rather flat open flowers.
CL TALISMAN CHT	Yellow, orange, and copper blend	M	A vigorous and prolific old favorite with the same perfect buds and glossy foliage as the bush form (described on page 48) with the bonus of good long cutting stems.
TEMPO P	Bright red	S	Pillar type or short climber, this is a bountiful producer of floribunda-like clusters. Individual blooms are very double and high-centered, opening from shapely deep red buds.
CL TROPICANA CHT (Photo on page 44)	Orange salmon	M	A garden magnet, its glowing color is impossible to overlook. Vigorous, producing blooms singly or in small clusters. May need watching for mildew.
WHITE DAWN LCL	Pure white	T	Medium-size, fragrant blooms have the form of a gardenia. Lavish spring display, moderate bloom through summer, then another big burst in fall. Vigorous; and cold tolerant to around 0°F/−18°C.

MINIATURES

Here is a selection of some of the highest-rated miniatures according to annual rating surveys conducted by The American Rose Society (see page 25). The designations for height are based upon relative heights plants would achieve when planted in the ground; short (S) is to 18 inches; medium (M) is 18–30 inches; tall (T) is more than 30 inches. When plants are grown in containers, the differences will be somewhat less pronounced.

RED & RED BICOLOR

BEAUTY SECRET, T. Lovely long-pointed buds open to semi-double blossoms. Dark green foliage. Photo, page 61.

DWARFKING, M. Deep velvety red, the well-formed buds open to cupped to flat, full-petaled flowers. Glossy foliage.

FIRE PRINCESS, M. Clusters of bright, fiery red orange blooms, both flowers and foliage larger than average.

(Continued on page 59)

Kassel   *Dortmund*

...Climbing Roses

Climbing Mrs. Sam McGredy

America

KATHY, M. Rich dark red, yet bright, well-formed double blossoms open from hybrid tealike buds. Photo, page 60.

LIBBY, M. Well-formed buds, in clusters and singly, open to semi-double flowers of white, heavily edged and shaded red. Photo, page 61.

MAGIC CARROUSEL, T. Striking combination of white petals precisely edged in red; shapely buds.

MY VALENTINE, S. Short, pointed buds; fairly small flowers in clusters; rosette-shaped rich red blossoms. Photo, page 60.

RED IMP, M. Plump buds open to double, flat flowers of velvety scarlet. Upright, compact, with small foliage.

ROBIN, S. Small cherry red blossoms—globular buds and pointed petal tips. A rounded, compact bush.

SCARLET GEM, M. Unfading bright scarlet flowers full of petals packed into small, globular buds. Dark, glossy leaves.

TINY WARRIOR, T. Compact bush is upright and quite tall, but double blossoms are only about an inch across.

TOY CLOWN, M. Shapely buds are white, tipped with red; open blooms are white with cerise petal edges. Large foliage.

PINK

BABY BETSY McCALL, M. Semi-double, half-dollar-size flowers from hybrid tealike buds; compact plant.

BABY OPHELIA, S. Buds are plump and pointed, in small clusters or singly. Plant is quite compact.

BO PEEP, S. Small flowers of light pink with hybrid tealike buds. Small foliage and compact plant.

CAROL JEAN, M. Rounded buds, fully double flowers are deep pink; open blooms are half-dollar size. Large foliage.

ELEANOR, M. Rather upright plant with glossy leaves produces coral pink blooms from rounded buds.

JANNA, T. Petals are white on the outside and edged in pink; inside of petals is edged and infused with more pink.

JUDY FISCHER, M. Beautifully formed, rose pink buds open to half-dollar-size hybrid tea replicas. Photo, page 60.

JUNE TIME, S. Spreading, glossy-leaved bush bears light pink blooms with darker petal reverses. Globular buds.

KATHY ROBINSON, T. Pink on the inside, white on the outside; beautifully formed buds and flowers.

MARY ADAIR, M. Hybrid-tea-style buds and flowers of a color between pink and orange. Spreading plant.

OPAL JEWEL, S. Pointed buds and fairly small, fully double flowers are light pink. Spreading plant.

PEACHES 'N' CREAM, M. Beautiful buds and flowers of finest hybrid tea quality. On the large side for a miniature. Photo, page 61.

PEACHY, M. Plump, pointed buds open into medium-size double flowers of an even peach tone.

PINK MANDY, S. Cool pink, small flowers open from plump buds in clusters. Spreading, fairly compact plant.

PIXIE ROSE, M. Double rose pink blossoms, the color deeper in the center; shapely buds. Rounded plant.

ROSMARIN, M. Dark-centered light pink flowers develop from rounded buds into rosette-shaped blooms. Spreading plant. Photo, page 61.

TRINKET, S. Small flowers, foliage, and plant. Pointed buds; light pink, double blooms with pointed petals.

WILLIE WINKIE, S. Another small, fine-textured miniature. Globular buds, very double rose pink blossoms.

ORANGE & MULTICOLOR

ANYTIME, M. Soft coral orange color; single flowers, up to 2 inches across, open from long, pointed buds. Photo, page 60.

BABY DARLING, M. Fully double apricot to orange flowers, either in small clusters or singly. Photo, page 60.

BABY MASQUERADE, T. Hybrid tealike buds are yellow, but change to orange and red as flower opens and ages.

CHIPPER, M. Pink and orange tones in hybrid-tea-style bud that opens to half-dollar-size double blossom.

HULA GIRL, T. Pure bright orange, from the attractive buds to the open blooms of half-dollar size. Photo, page 60.

HUMDINGER, T. Hybrid tealike buds of light orange, and large double flowers, in clusters and on individual stems.

JEANNIE WILLIAMS, M. Basically yellow, but upper petal surfaces are infused with orange red. Attractive small buds.

MARY MARSHALL, T. Larger than average flowers open from flawless buds; orange, but with tints of red and yellow.

ORANGE HONEY, M. Perfectly shaped, golden orange buds which take on red tones as flowers open and age. Photo, page 61.

PERSIAN PRINCESS, T. The color of hybrid tea 'Tropicana' (see page 44) in a large-flowered, tall miniature.

SHERI ANNE, M. Lovely buds in a brilliant color: more orange than 'Starina'. Semi-double blooms; spreading plant.

STARINA, M. Faultless buds and open flowers of best hybrid-tea-style. Vivid, long-lasting blooms; glossy foliage. Photo, page 61.

YELLOW

GOLD COIN, S. Compact bush with small, light green foliage and shapely bright yellow buds on individual stems.

RISE 'N' SHINE, M. Beautifully shaped golden buds open into large flowers, many on individual stems. Large foliage.

YELLOW DOLL, S. Beautiful buds are pure, glowing yellow, opening to fairly large, double flowers. Short and spreading. Photo, page 61.

WHITE

CINDERELLA, M. Small foliage and compact, bushy plant. Small buds; 1-inch double blooms are palest pink in cool weather.

EASTER MORNING, M. Ivory white, the globular buds open to double blooms up to 2 inches across. Glossy foliage.

PIXIE, S. Small, double flowers sometimes tinted pink. Tiny, fine-textured foliage on low, spreading, compact bush.

POPCORN, M. Globular buds pop open to clusters of tiny, semi-double flowers. Rounded plant. Photo, page 60.

SIMPLEX, S. Open flowers, are major attraction. Each bloom is starlike, 5-petaled single, to half-dollar size.

STARGLO, T. White buds open to double blooms with a "glo" of cream and with pointed petal tips (the "star").

LAVENDER

LAVENDER LACE, M. Close to color of hybrid tea 'Sterling Silver' (see page 53). Blooms mostly in clusters; spreading plant.

My Valentine

My Valentine   *Popcorn*

Hula Girl

Miniature Roses

**embodying the beauty
of their larger kin**

(All miniatures shown are half size to full size)

Kathy   *Anytime*

Judy Fischer

Baby Darling

Libby

Beauty Secret

Rosmarin

Orange Honey

Peaches 'n' Cream

Starina

Yellow Doll

The Art of Growing Roses

Roses thrive in a variety of soils. This fact underscores one of the plant's virtues: rugged adaptability. Yet the roots of a rose plant do have a few definite preferences that, when satisfied, can make the difference between indifferent and superior performance. Before you plant your new roses you should know these preferences, what *your* soil is like, and how it can be handled to satisfy the roses' needs.

WHAT KIND OF SOIL DO YOU HAVE?

All soil is composed of mineral particles formed by the action of weather on some sort of rock. These particles do not fit together exactly—there are pore spaces between them. When soil is dry, the spaces are filled with air; but when water is added to soil, it moves downward, filling the spaces with water and coating each particle. As water continues to move down through soil, air re-enters the spaces vacated by water, though a water film remains around each soil grain.

This interchange between water and air in the soil is vital to rose roots. In order to reach their best possible growth, roses need a soil that is moist but that drains well enough that the soil's natural air spaces do not remain filled with water for any length of time. Roots need oxygen to function; in a waterlogged soil the oxygen supply is cut off and the roots suffocate.

Without going into a detailed breakdown of soil classification, let's consider that most soils will be basically clay, sand, or some gradation between the two. What determines whether it's a clayey or sandy soil is the size of its individual particles.

Clay soils are composed of minute, flattened particles that group together very tightly, producing a compact, "heavy" soil. Pore spaces between clay particles are microscopic; water drains very slowly through them and air space is severely limited. Despite the fact that individual clay particles are well supplied with nutrients essential for plant growth, plant roots have a difficult time penetrating in this compact soil.

Sandy soils contain the largest particles (more than 25 times the size of the largest clay particles) and have correspondingly large pore spaces. They drain well (so are well aerated) but retain moisture and dissolved nutrients so poorly that plants need more frequent attention than they do when planted in clay.

Loam, the happy medium so often mentioned in garden books, may contain soil particles intermediate in size between clay and sand, and/or may contain a mixture of particle sizes. The drainage, aeration, and moisture retention of loam also represent a compromise between the extremes of clay and sand.

Drainage test. How can you tell what sort of soil you have? You can look, feel, and dig. Clay soils usually will crack when dry; sandy ones won't. When wet, clays can feel almost greasy, but sand will feel gritty. Finally, dig about a foot-deep hole and fill it with water; if there still is water in the hole an hour later, you can be sure your soil is more clayey than sandy and probably will require some special attention to improve its drainage (see page 65).

How deep is your soil?

You should have no trouble discovering whether your soil tends to be sandy, clayey, or somewhere in between. The next determination you'll have to make

PERIODIC APPLICATIONS of fertilizer (see pages 74–78) encourage growth and bloom. Here a husky plant of floribunda 'Sarabande' receives fertilizer as one bloom cycle is on the wane.

is the depth of your soil. Take a spade or spading fork and dig a trial hole about 2 feet deep in the area where you want to plant your roses. With any luck, you will encounter no obstruction—and neither will rose roots. Complications you might encounter close to the soil surface are these: hardpan (a layer of impervious soil, usually found only in low-rainfall regions), bedrock (or at least the parent material of your soil, such as limestone or sandstone), or occasional boulders too large to remove.

Where a hardpan prevails, you sometimes can break through (if it is not too thick) and laboriously but successfully remove it from a planting bed. Often beneath it will be subsoil that will drain adequately. With bedrock near the surface, you'll have to construct raised planting beds; these, with the combined depth of native topsoil and new soil added to the bed, should provide about a 2-foot depth for your roses' roots.

Sometimes soil around new homes may have been compacted by heavy equipment used in construction. It also may contain quantities of construction debris (especially close to the house). A deep digging (with the aeration it brings) plus incorporation of organic materials may be all you'll need to do in a light to medium soil. With compacted heavy clay soil, though, it probably would be easier and more effective for you to make raised planting beds.

Improving your soil

Knowing your basic soil type gives you the theme upon which you make the variations to best satisfy your roses. And a component that can beneficially vary all soils is organic matter—decomposing plant and animal remains.

In clay soils, organic materials act as wedges between the tiny, compacted soil particles while the more fully decomposed parts of the organic matter (called *humus*) are sticky and hold together groups of soil particles to make small crumbs. This wedging and gathering action loosens up the clay and allows freer penetration of air and water. In sandy soils, organic materials fill in the spaces between sand grains and act as sponges to hold moisture and nutrients, reducing the too-rapid drainage. And keep in mind the human benefit of added organic matter: it makes it easier for you, the gardener, to dig and cultivate.

You have a wide choice of organic materials that will improve your soil. The easiest (but more expensive) to get are commercially packaged items such as peat moss, steer manure, redwood sawdust, or leaf mold. Very likely you will be able to locate suitable waste materials in your area—inexpensive if you are able to haul them away. Grape or apple pomace, rice hulls, ground corncobs, wood by-products such as sawdust and shavings, mushroom compost, spent hops, and various animal manures are just a small sampling of materials you might find. If you maintain a compost pile, you need not search beyond your own back yard.

Whatever you add to improve your soil, try to use enough to comprise at least 25 percent of the amount of soil you're preparing. This means that for the average spade's depth bite (8–9 inches), ideally you should add about 3 inches of organic material. For easier work and more uniform results, dig in not more than a 2-inch layer of organic materials at one time. If you don't plan to improve the soil of the entire rose bed but prefer to add organic materials to each hole at planting time, be sure to read the cautions mentioned under "Steps toward better drainage," page 65. In addition, remember that a planting hole well fortified with organic matter can be a trap if surrounding soil is poorly drained; each hole becomes a suffocating bathtub for roots.

If you have a clay soil, consider two other widely sold and relatively inexpensive materials you can add in addition to organic matter to improve the soil structure. Both gypsum and lime, when added to clay, will cause the particles to group together into larger crumbs, improving drainage and workability. Which one you use depends upon the acidity or alkalinity of your soil (see "Soil Testing," page 76). If you have neutral to alkaline soil, use gypsum; sprinkle it on the soil surface so that it resembles a light snowfall, then dig it in. For acid soils, use lime in the amount recommended by your County Cooperative Extension Advisor (or agricultural advisor). Remember roses perform best in soils that fall in the range between slightly acid and slightly alkaline (roughly *p*H 6.5–7.2).

Why prepare early?

If you know several months in advance that you are going to plant roses, you have the opportunity to prepare soil early so that it will have a chance to mellow and settle in the meantime. This also makes the planting more pleasurable when the roses arrive: you then don't have to spend time adding organic components to the soil while the roses wait. For fall planting, prepare your soil in summer; but if you will be planting in winter or spring, see that you prepare your soil in early fall at the latest. After you have spaded and incorporated organic matter, the soil level will be several inches above the surrounding soil, but by the time rose planting season arrives it will have settled so that you can easily gauge the proper planting depth.

Advance preparation gives you the chance to use a much greater variety of organic soil amendments than you could use at the time you plant your roses. Fresh animal manures (which will burn newly planted rose roots with their excessive nitrogen content) and undecomposed organic materials (which temporarily take nitrogen from the soil to aid their breakdown) usually will mellow sufficiently within several months after having been added to the soil so that you can then plant with safety.

If you choose to improve the soil at the time you

plant new roses, be sure to use organic materials that contain enough nitrogen for their decomposition (such as nitrogen-fortified wood products), or materials that already are significantly decomposed (compost or leaf mold, for example), or peat moss, which breaks down so slowly that there is no significant nitrogen depletion. Don't risk using animal manure in a planting hole where it would come into direct contact with roots unless you are sure the manure is thoroughly aged.

Steps toward better drainage

If your soil has flunked the "drainage test" (page 62), you would be wise to make some special preparations for the planting area before you begin to improve the soil. Even the most ideal, porous soil will not grow roses well if the subsoil and soil surrounding the bed are of heavy clay that will not allow water to escape from the area. Without making provisions for drainage away from the site, you essentially plant your roses in undrained containers.

What should you do for poorly drained soil? If your garden is level, a raised bed is your best solution. Plan to have the soil surface of the raised bed 1 foot above the normal grade. Dig organic materials and gypsum or lime (see "Improving your soil," page 64) into the top 2 feet of native soil, then add the additional soil to raise the bed and dig it (along with more organic matter) into the native soil beneath. Allow a couple of months for the bed to settle before you plant it. If settling is too great, add more new soil.

Where soil is poorly drained and the garden is on a slope (or if land near the proposed planting site slopes away from it), you can plant at ground level if you install drainage pipes or tile beneath the beds. Then, when water passes down through the carefully prepared rose bed soil, it enters the pipes and moves out of the bed, *if* it can empty into a spot lower than the level of the pipe—either by draining downslope or by draining into a sump.

Installation of pipe is simply an efficient modification of an ancient drainage principle: Roman swampland was drained for cultivation by the digging of deep and broad trenches to collect water that saturated the top several feet of soil. The diagram below shows how to place the drainage pipes. After the pipes are in place, prepare the soil above them with organic materials, gypsum or lime (see "Improving your soil," page 64); then let the soil settle before planting.

If the slope of your land is not a gentle one, you might prefer to terrace your plantings. This will give you a level planting surface, yet water will drain away down the slope. Wood, concrete blocks, brick, or even stone (if you're ambitious and skillful) all make fine retaining walls for terraced beds. Build the retaining walls first, then fill in behind with soil liberally mixed with organic materials. Especially if your native soil drains poorly, you'd be wise to incorporate several "weep holes" at the base of each retaining wall; these will allow excess water to drain easily out of the bed instead of collecting at the lowest part and building up pressure against the retaining wall.

Planting in problem sites

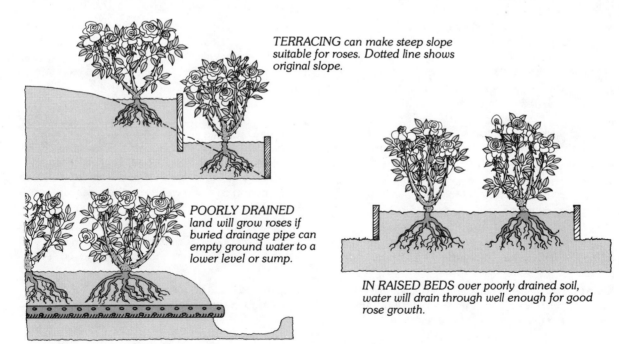

TERRACING can make steep slope suitable for roses. Dotted line shows original slope.

POORLY DRAINED land will grow roses if buried drainage pipe can empty ground water to a lower level or sump.

IN RAISED BEDS over poorly drained soil, water will drain through well enough for good rose growth.

Older gardening books—particularly those from England—describe a laborious but *effective* way to prepare soil deeply. Called double digging, it aerates and improves the subsoil—from about the 12-inch to the 24-inch depth. Since rose roots can (and should) penetrate deeply, this sort of soil preparation is to their advantage. However, there is a *reasonably* simple way to do it—at least a less cumbersome method than that recommended by English gardeners. First dig out the top foot of soil from the proposed rose bed and lay this soil to one side (put it on some sort of tarpaulin or plastic cloth if you have to pile it on lawn or a loose paving material). Then, thoroughly dig into the next foot of soil your organic materials (and gypsum or lime if your soil needs it). Finally, return to the bed the soil you had laid aside, digging into this top layer the same materials you just have added to the subsoil.

SHOPPING WISELY FOR ROSES

Now that you understand your soil and have made any necessary adjustments so that it should grow roses well, you can concentrate on selecting and purchasing the plants. And because all roses are not alike in growth habit and area adaptability (not to mention color differences), you will want to devote some time to selecting just the right rose varieties for your garden (see "Which varieties to choose," below). Then you can consider whether you will want to send for the plants from a mail-order specialist or shop locally—at nurseries or supermarkets for bare-root plants during the dormant season or, when plants are in bloom, from the container-grown selections at retail nurseries or garden centers (see "Bare-root or container-grown," and "Where to buy roses," pages 67–69).

Which varieties to choose

Most roses will grow in nearly any climate, but some varieties do better than others in particular regions. For your greatest pleasure you should first find out what sorts perform well in your area, and one of the best sources of this information is a local rose grower. Even conversations with your neighbors may disclose at least a limited list of sure performers for your area. Many towns have public gardens and specific rose test gardens where newer varieties plus satisfactory old favorites are displayed. Often, visits to one of these gardens will show you which varieties are suited to

A Few Rose Terms to Know

As you read about roses, you are bound to run across terms that have special meaning when applied to rose growing. The following list explains the most familiar jargon words of the rose world.

Bud. This may have several meanings. The most obvious is reference to the unopened flower. It also can mean the growth bud or eye found where leaves join stems. For a propagator of roses, to *bud* is to take the growth eye and develop a plant from it by a special grafting technique (see page 93).

Bud union. On a commercially propagated rose bush, this is the part of the plant where top growth joins with the understock (below right), generally 1–3 inches above the roots. It is an enlarged "knob" from which all major stems grow (and it grows larger each year).

Canes. The principal stems which grow from the bud union (or from very low on the bush) and form the plant's structure.

Hip. The seed pod that can form after a flower's petals fall if the bloom was pollinated (as happens naturally very often). Many turn brilliant autumn colors.

Plant patent. Most new rose introductions are "patented." This means that the patent holder and the rose's originator receive a small percentage from the sale of each plant until the patent expires after 17 years. This is a strong guarantee that plants you purchase will be true to name and well grown. It also stimulates research and hybridizing, as the hybridizer is assured of some financial reward for his work.

Sport. A change in growth habit or flower color that may occur suddenly on an established variety. Climbing forms of bush varieties typify a growth sport; 'Flaming Peace,' a red and gold bicolor, is an example of a color sport which was found on a plant of the normally light yellow and pink 'Peace.'

Standard. Commonly called "tree rose," the standard is just a rose bush budded high on an understock stem (see page 85). Sizes range from miniature standards on 12-inch stems through 24-inch patio standards, 36-inch regular standards to occasional 6-foot weeping standards featuring flexible-caned ramblers.

Sucker. Any growth that arises from below the bud union on a budded plant. This growth is that of the understock and should be removed (see page 87).

Understock. The rose that furnished the root system to plants propagated by budding (see page 93).

your climate. For vital statistics on 267 rose varieties (and color photographs of 82 favorites), browse through pages 26-61.

For a list of AARS accredited public rose gardens in the United States and Canada, write to All-America Rose Selections, P.O. Box 218, Shenandoah, IA 51610.

Bare-root or container-grown

Roses are available throughout the year for garden planting: dormant bare-root bushes during the late fall to early spring dormant season, and growing bushes in containers of soil during the warmer months of the year. Each mode of availability has advantages and drawbacks, detailed below.

Bare root. The majority of rose plants marketed annually are dormant bare-root specimens, available from mail-order specialists, retail nurseries, garden centers, and even at some supermarkets. In this dormant state, the plants must only be kept from extremes in temperature and from drying out. Mail-order suppliers keep plants sufficiently moist for shipment by enclosing them in polyethylene plastic bags or encasing the roots in a moistened lightweight material such as sawdust. Retail nurseries may hold quantities of bare-root bushes heeled-in in beds of sawdust; supermarkets and some nurseries will offer plants individually root-wrapped in a moistened fibrous material.

The primary disadvantage to bare-root roses relates to the gardener's convenience: such roses are available for planting during the least appealing time of year for gardening. But to many gardeners, the bare-root advantages far outweigh the possible discomfort. A bare-root plant will cost less than will the same variety grown to flowering size and sold in a container. A much greater choice of varieties is available bare-root than container-grown. And a bare-root plant is easier to plant. See pages 69–71 for specific planting directions.

Container-grown roses. Throughout the year many retail nurseries have selections of roses growing and blooming in containers. Generally these plants are more expensive than the same varieties bare-root because of the labor required to plant and care for them at the nursery.

Of the several advantages to buying these roses, perhaps the most compelling one is that you can see that the plant is alive and healthy and you can check its flowers (especially important if the variety is new to you). You will be able to tell if its color and form are what you prefer, and you can tell something about its foliage color and disease resistance. If any roses in your garden have died over the winter, this is a quick way to fill in the gaps; and, of course, it puts instant color into a new rose garden. The best time to go shopping for container-grown roses is during their first flush of bloom in spring, since flowers are often at their best then and the selection of varieties will be greatest.

What, then, are the risks in buying container-grown roses? As with packaged supermarket plants, you cannot see the root systems. But here you *can* see and judge the plant's health and vigor, and almost always you will be correct in assuming that the container plant is just as healthy beneath the soil surface.

Unless the nursery specializes in container-grown roses, you probably will find the selection more limited than the bare-root offering.

If you go shopping for blooming roses in containers, keep these three points in mind:

• Purchase only bushes that were planted earlier in the year from bare-root stock, except for miniature and micropropagated plants. Under nursery conditions, container-grown roses held over from previous years inevitably suffer from their prolonged confinement. Tell-tale signs of such older plants are pruning scars from past years (often accompanied by dieback below the cuts) or dead canes or branches with twiggy growth attached.

• Buy your roses in the largest container offered. The best are 3 or 5-gallon cans or their equivalent volume in wooden tubs, crates, or paper pots. Former bare-root roses in gallon cans or small flower pots may have been root-pruned to fit into the small containers.

• Do your shopping before summer heat arrives. Not only do nursery roses look their worst then, but also summer is the most difficult time of year to establish a new plant in your garden.

[**Micropropagation.** *The practice of propagating plants from individual cells under laboratory conditions (popularly called "tissue culture") is now part of commercial rose production. Many of these laboratory-started plants are then field-grown and harvested for the bare-root season. These plants are unique in that they grow on their own roots rather than an understock, and their roots are more fibrous and plentiful than the familiar budded-plant roots. Some of these laboratory-started plants are available in small pots during the growing season; plant them in well-prepared soil, as you would plant potted annuals or perennials. Within a year, they will become husky, well-rooted bushes.*]

Where to buy roses

Avoiding the temptation to buy roses is not easy. Most nurseries promote them throughout the year: first in bare-root form during the planting season, then in containers during the remaining months. Large commercial rose growers advertise their wares widely with enticing color photographs. And if you escape these inducements, very likely you may be drawn to the packaged bare-root plants offered for sale in supermarkets. You may wonder which sources will give you the best plants for your money—and the answer is that any of them *can*. What you have to

Bare-root Quality Standards

Nearly all roses sold bare-root are "2-year-old, field-grown plants." This means that the roots are about 2 years old and the canes somewhat younger. For these bare-root plants, the American Association of Nurserymen has established quality standards, designated by numbers. Consequently, when a nursery advertises No. 1, No. 1½, or No. 2 plants, you know in advance what sort of plants to expect. For the principal types of roses sold—hybrid tea, grandiflora, floribunda, polyantha, and climber—here are the specifications for these grades; in all cases, the canes measured to determine the grade should originate within 3 inches of the bud union where top growth joins understock.

No. 1 grade. Hybrid teas and grandifloras must have three or more strong canes, at least two of which are 18 inches or more in length. Canes on No. 1 floribundas should meet the same specifications, except that they need be only 15 inches long. Number 1 polyanthas must have four or more canes of 12 inches or longer. Climbing roses need three or more canes of at least 24 inches.

No 1½ grade. Hybrid teas and grandifloras need two or more strong canes of at least 15 inches long. Floribundas should have two canes that measure 14 inches or more. Number 1½ climbers must have two 18-inch canes. Polyanthas that do not meet number 1 standards are not graded.

No. 2 grade. Hybrid teas, grandifloras, and climbers—the only types you're ever likely to find in this grade—need have only two canes of 12 inches or longer. These plants are strictly a gamble, since they may be the runts of the 2-year-old field which produced the No. 1 plants also being offered.

Measurements expressed in the grading standards are for the plant as it is dug from the field. Very often the grower, packager, or nurseryman will reduce the cane length for more convenient shipping or handling, but you can tell from the cane diameter whether the plant originally qualified for the grade indicated. Some of the smaller-growing roses (such as 'Sarabande') may appear to just barely make the No. 1 standards, but this size is natural: never will they have canes equal to those of husky giants like 'Queen Elizabeth'.

---

do is consider the advantages and drawbacks in each situation.

Mail order. If you purchase from a mail-order rose-specialist nursery, your only disadvantage is that you can't personally select the plants you receive. But because their business depends entirely on your satisfaction, they will ship nothing but first class plants. Aside from convenience (you just wait for the plants to come to you), mail-order rose specialists are the readiest sources for the newest hybrids. Some of these nurseries also make a point of carrying old or unusual roses that are seldom available locally (see page 14). The mail-order catalogs usually offer a greater selection from which to choose than any other source; but they may not always carry the middle-aged and old-favorite hybrid teas whose low individual prices can't justify producing them in quantity and allocating to them color catalog space.

Catalog shopping can be a truly exciting experience. The descriptions—if not sufficiently tantalizing in themselves—often will be accompanied by irresistible color photographs. In your eagerness to throw all caution to the winds and send for *every* rose you want, keep in mind the guidelines outlined on page 66 for

selecting satisfactory varieties for your area.

Although planting times vary from fall through spring (see page 69–71) throughout the country, the earlier you place your order the more certain you are of receiving your first choices. Most catalogs are ready for mailing sometime in the fall. No matter when you plant, you would be wise to place your order soon after catalogs arrive—ideally before the December holidays. Ask for delivery of plants early in your region's bare-root planting season. This will give new plants the longest possible growing season in your garden, and is good insurance that your choices won't be sold out. If, however, you find yourself placing a late order, you are likely to be happier if you list a few acceptable substitutions rather than leave the choice of possible alternates to the seller. This way you avoid receiving as a substitute a rose you already have or one you don't care for. Many large mail-order rose growers (even those in warm-winter areas) have cold-storage facilities that enable them to ship you well-ripened, dormant bushes at the best planting time for your region.

Nurseries. The particular roses stocked by your nearby nursery depend on who does the buying and stocking, but typically you will find the new and recent All-America winners (see page 26) as well as the standard, time-tested, and proven varieties. In addition, you're almost certain to find any roses that are especially suited to your regional climate, regardless of their performance in other dissimilar areas. Usually, the bare-root roses will be heeled into beds of sawdust so that you can pick out plants having good, healthy canes. This way, if you see that a plant's root system has been badly damaged in digging or shipping, you can select another one on the spot. Since the nursery owner's livelihood depends on return business and word-of-mouth endorsement, the interest in your satisfaction is great.

Supermarkets. Perhaps the source of greatest concern is the local supermarket. For convenience it can't be beaten. Although the assortment of varieties will not be exceptional, typically they will be the old favorites of past decades as well as current top-rated patented roses. Sometimes a disappointingly high percentage of these roses is incorrectly labeled. Unfortunately, there's no sure way to determine this until they leaf out and bloom. So if you are looking for a particular variety, you have a much better chance for satisfaction from mail-order specialists or retail nurseries. But the chief problem with plants from the local supermarket is that you can't see their root systems. Inevitably the roots are enclosed in long, narrow bags containing a moistened fibrous material, the bag tied just below the bud union. The canes are always on view—either dipped in wax to retain moisture or swathed in a transparent plastic bag for the same reason. Assuming the canes appear in good condition—not shriveled or discolored, eyes plump and ready to grow but not growing—you can consider the plant a good risk. Sometimes in the digging or in the packaging, however, major roots will be broken, and you won't discover this until you unwrap them just before planting. Such roses may take an extra year or two, while they rebuild their lost root systems, before showing their best in your garden.

One general tip for buying packaged rose plants: do it while they are still *new* on the supermarket shelves. Those with plastic-wrapped canes are well protected against the drying indoor atmosphere, but because the plastic acts as a miniature greenhouse, these plants often begin to grow soon after being set out on the shelves. Even if you're not prepared to plant them as soon as they appear in the market, *you* can more carefully watch over the packaged roses at home until you're ready to plant. If you can't plant them right away, see "Holding methods for plants" on this page.

Should you, despite all precautions, find yourself with sprouted plants to set out, just cut the shoots back to ¼-inch stubs. This will prevent the new shoots from using up moisture in the plants before roots are established enough to replenish it.

PLANTING—PREPARATIONS AND PROCEDURES

Before you even pick up a shovel, examine your new bushes carefully. They should measure up to the grade advertised by the seller (see page 68) and not appear weak or spindly; the root system should not have been badly cut up in the harvesting or broken in shipping. Sometimes you will find slight root breakage in packaging and shipping, but it should not be excessive. Always cut back any damaged roots with a sharp, clean pair of pruning shears before you plant.

Occasionally, plants shipped during severe winter weather become frozen in transit. Freezing breaks up the cell structure of the canes and usually causes the roots to turn black. Even if you carefully thaw them, these plants are practically worthless and should be replaced. Plants that have been overheated in transit will have live roots but black canes. Very rarely will you receive a diseased or dead plant.

Any time the quality of the plants you receive does not measure up to what you expected, you immediately should get in touch with the nursery or mail-order specialist about possible replacement. But give the seller the benefit of the doubt. Reputable rose specialists and nursery workers are eager to see that you get top quality stock and often they will replace plants, even when damage was beyond their control.

Holding methods for plants

When weather and soil conditions permit, the ideal moment to plant new roses is as soon as you get them. If you cannot plant right away, you should do one of two things to keep the new arrivals in a fresh but dormant condition until you can plant:

1) Heeling-in—the simplest and best treatment for holding new roses—is possible only when you are able to work the soil. In a shaded place, dig a trench that has one slanted side; lay the plants against this slant with their roots at the trench's bottom, then cover the roots *and* canes with soil, thoroughly watering them in. In a cool shaded spot, these roses will hold longer before breaking dormancy than they would where exposed to warming sunlight. Even so, you should plant them at the very first opportunity, for root growth may begin while heeled in, and the less of this there is to disturb during planting, the better.

2) An alternate method, whenever heeling-in is impossible, is to pack the roots in some sort of moisture-retentive material and set new plants in a cool (but not freezing) place, such as a garage or basement. Very often mail-order roses and even plants from the nearby nursery will have their roots packed in moist peat moss, sawdust, perlite, or similar absorbent material. All you have to do, then, is remove the

Bare-root planting steps

In the procedures for bare-root rose planting, shown below, nothing has aroused more controversy over the years than the question of how high or low to position the rose's bud union. For years, cold-winter rosarians planted their bushes with bud unions 1 to 2 inches below the soil surface, to ensure winter insulation. In contrast, mild-climate rose growers would plant with bud unions even with the soil surface or raised an inch or so above it, claiming that more new canes were produced when the bud union was exposed. Current practice favors planting with bud unions even with the soil surface in all climates, carefully applying winter protection (see pages 88–90) in climates that require it. This positioning allows for good growth from the plant's base and, in time, may encourage roots to form from the bud union as well.

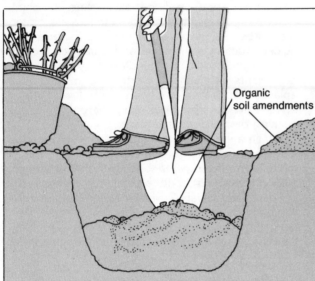

DIG PLANTING HOLE large enough to hold rose roots without crowding or bending; mix in soil amendments.

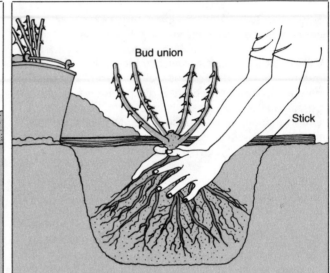

FORM A FIRM CONE of soil in hole, spread roots over cone. Stick across hole shows level of surrounding soil, lets you accurately position bud union.

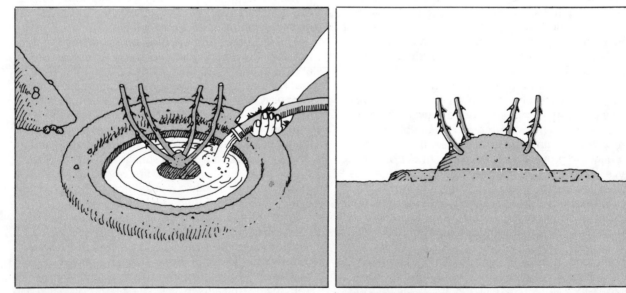

FILL SOIL IN around roots, firming it as you go with your hands or a stick. Thoroughly water plant in, making sure it doesn't settle below established level.

MOUND MOIST SOIL over bud union and lower part of canes. Keep mound moist until new growth begins, then carefully remove.

packing, soak it in water, squeeze out surplus moisture so it is damp but doesn't drip, and repack it around the rose roots. Check these plants often to make sure the packing does not dry out, and add more water if necessary.

Some roses may come to you completely encased in plastic bags or sheeting that retain moisture well around roots and canes. If you leave the bags unopened and keep them in a cool, dark place, they will hold safely for a week to 10 days. But if you have to hold these plants indoors where it is warmer, be sure to remove the plastic from around the canes; moisture will condense on the inside of the plastic and, combined with warmth, can make miniature greenhouses out of the package and cause the plants to start growth. In this case you will need to get some peat moss, sawdust, or other moisture-holding material to pack around the roots.

Whatever holding method you use, don't let the rose roots dry out, even for a short time.

With any bare-root rose bush, it is a good idea to soak the entire plant in water for a few hours (but not more than 24) just before planting. This will help restore moisture to all the plant tissues at once. Then, after you plant, cover the canes with a mound of moist soil or other moisture-holding material for a week or two to keep canes from drying while the roots are establishing themselves. Gradually and carefully remove this mound as new growth begins.

When to do bare-root planting

Technically, you can plant bare-root roses at any time during the dormant season when soil is not frozen. For much of the South, Southwest, and West Coast, this means January and February, with the possibility of March before dormancy is broken. In these regions, where winter lows seldom reach 10°F/−12 °C, the sooner you can plant, the better.

In other parts of the country where winter cold is capricious—alternating with spells of warmer weather—and where freezing typically settles in for several months, you probably will prefer (if not be compelled) to plant either in fall or spring. The one advantage to fall planting is that the new plant may have about a 5-month lead over the spring-planted bush in establishing its roots. In severe winters, though, little if any root growth will take place, and you run a risk of losing a new plant even though you protect it well. A premature spring warm spell may be just enough to break a new plant's dormancy and leave it vulnerable to subsequent freezes. The only real drawback to spring planting is that top growth and root growth begin almost simultaneously. If early spring weather is unseasonably warm, the top may temporarily outstrip the roots. These plants will need close attention to be sure roots always have enough water.

In cold-winter areas, experienced growers in your region can give you the best advice for local planting time. Rose-growing friends, a reliable nurseryman who deals in roses, or the nearest Consulting Rosarian (see page 25) should be able to advise you well. Generally, if you are ordering from a large specialist rose nursery that has cold storage facilities, you'd be wise to order for early spring planting; the grower can hold the new bushes over the winter under ideal conditions.

WATERING

There is no mystery involved in watering roses. Yet a lack of sufficient water probably is the major cause of unsatisfactory results from roses—especially newly planted ones. The rose is a thirsty plant. Although the bushes usually will survive when only skimpily supplied with water, they will perform at their vigorous best only when their roots are kept moist during the growing season. Even in regions where spring and summer rainfall is frequent, don't assume that these showers will completely satisfy your roses' needs.

A frequently quoted rule of thumb is that roses need at least 1 inch of rainfall, or its equivalent, per week. This oversimplifies the water question although it does highlight the roses' preference for ample water and a cool root zone. More precisely, the amount of water that roses should receive can be stated only in relation to the kind of soil you have. First, remember that although rose roots should be kept damp, the soil around them should never be saturated for any length of time. Such saturation keeps vital oxygen from the soil (see page 62), and roots need oxygen as much as they do water in order to carry on the plant's life processes.

Watering to the full depth of their roots will produce the best results from your roses. This means a water penetration to at least 16-18 inches. Frequent but light waterings will not penetrate very far below the soil surface. This encourages the network of feeder roots to grow in this shallow, moist zone. Concentrated close to the surface, these roots are subject to injury by cultivating or weeding, may be burned by fertilizers, or may be damaged if the surface soil layer dries out.

But how can you tell if your watering has penetrated deeply enough? The surest way is to conduct a simple test to determine your soil's ability to absorb water; you can time subsequent water applications to match your soil's capacity. Begin by watering your roses as you normally would (or, if you are growing your first roses, pick an arbitrary amount of time—say, 15 minutes). Then, on the day after you water, dig down about 18 inches to actually see how far your watering penetrated. If you discover, for example, that 30 minutes of irrigation wet only the top 10 inches of soil, you will know that your watering time should be increased in order to moisten the entire root zone.

Since water penetration varies according to soil type, the University of California conducted studies to accurately determine rates of absorption in the different types. These studies disclosed that 1 cubic inch of water on top of the ground will wet directly downward 12 inches in sandy soil, 6-10 inches in loam, or 4-5 inches in clay. This means that to wet the soil to a 2-foot depth in a 2-foot-square basin requires 5 gallons of water in a sandy soil, 7.6 gallons in loam, and 13.2 gallons in clay. Few people would want to take the time to water their roses by the gallon, but these figures point out that a trickle from the hose in clay soil will take a longer time to produce the necessary penetration than will the same flow in sand.

After asking how much water roses need, the next question to ask is how often they should be watered. And here again the answer is a relative one, depending on your soil. As the University of California studies imply, sandy soil absorbs water quickly whereas clay soils are slow to take it in. Water is exhausted much more quickly, however, in sand than in clay. In sandy soil, then, you will spend fewer hours at a time watering your roses than you would in clay, but you'll return to do it more often. For example, during "average" spring-time weather you may have to water your roses about every 5 days in sand, every week to week-and-a-half in loam, but only every other week in clay. Daytime temperatures, amount of sunlight, and wind action—all of which influence the transpiration rate—as well as the amount of rainfall and the presence or lack of a mulch will vary these generalizations.

An easy way to check the need for water is to take a trowel and open up a small hole in the soil, then feel with your finger to see if the soil is moist (not soggy) 3 inches below the surface. If it is damp, wait; but if the soil is dry, water again for your usual amount of time.

If you live in a summer-rainfall region, a rain gauge placed in your rose bed (but out of reach of any sprinklers) will give you a fairly accurate—and perhaps surprising—record of how much or little water nature is providing.

Don't overlook dormant-season watering, just because your roses are standing still. Continue to water, but on a more limited program, as long as the soil is not frozen.

How to apply water

When it comes to *how* to water your roses, you have a choice between irrigating and sprinkling. Most successful rose growers in summer-rainfall regions will vote for some form of irrigation as the better choice. There, rain washes foliage often enough, but may not be enough to keep roots moist. In dry-summer areas, many rosarians get best results from regular irrigation augmented by periodic sprinklings of the entire rose garden.

Particularly in smoggy or dusty areas, you will do your plants a great favor if you wash off their foliage every week or so. (As an added bonus this also will wash away some insect pests, notably aphids and spider mites.) But for this, pick an early morning of what promises to be a sunny day, so that leaves will be dry by nightfall.

You can provide a simple basin around each plant or elaborate systems of canals that link all basins together. But best results usually follow when each plant has its own basin so that irrigation water can be concentrated in the plant's root zone. The basic basin is simply an earthen dike 2 to 6 inches high around each plant; make it about 20 inches or more across. Its rim should encircle the bush just beyond the drip line (or the anticipated drip line of a newly planted bush). For established plantings, don't try to make the basin ridges by scraping soil from the rose bed. Instead, bring in enough soil from another part of the garden. Any disturbance of the soil surface near the rose plant could damage some of its feeder roots which lie just beneath the soil surface.

If you think a rose planting will be unattractive with each bush growing out of a separate crater-like basin, you can modify this effect by using a mulch (see page 73) inside the basins and on the ground between.

You can create a more formal, structured appearance by making the basin sides of brick or concrete block. This is particularly useful in sandy soils which cannot compact well enough to make very stable ridges, but it is useful anywhere you want a basin whose sides will never need repair. If your native soil is stony, you could employ some of the larger stones to make naturalistic basins that will be as permanent as brick or concrete. Gardeners in arid regions where flood irrigation is employed for all plants often entirely surround their rose beds with a concrete curbing to contain the water.

Watering roses in basins presents a very minor efficiency problem. With just a few bushes, the simplest method is to move the hose from plant to plant until all are watered. You can reduce the time this takes by employing one or more "Y" connections at the end of your principal hose, with secondary hoses going to more than one bush at a time. To avoid having soil scoured by water from the hose end, you can buy a "bubbler" attachment that diffuses the water through many small holes to reduce its force without cutting down the volume. An old sock or garden glove tied over the hose end accomplishes the same purpose.

If you want to water many bushes at once, or even just a few, you can put together a watering system from plastic pipe or tubing. This is simple and very successful. You just get fittings that will let you connect a garden hose to the system to supply water, and thus eliminate any need for direct connection to your outdoor plumbing.

Rigid plastic pipe can be used to create a sprinkling

Simple irrigation schemes

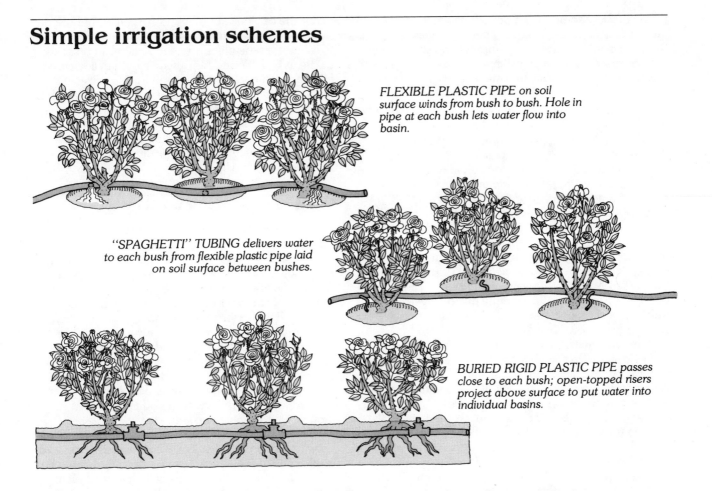

FLEXIBLE PLASTIC PIPE on soil surface winds from bush to bush. Hole in pipe at each bush lets water flow into basin.

"SPAGHETTI" TUBING delivers water to each bush from flexible plastic pipe laid on soil surface between bushes.

BURIED RIGID PLASTIC PIPE passes close to each bush; open-topped risers project above surface to put water into individual basins.

or irrigation system. You cut the pipe with a saw and make all connections with plastic fittings and special glue or metal clamps (depending on the type of plastic pipe used). But the flexible black plastic tubing designed for drip irrigation is far easier and quicker to work with. You can cut it with pruning shears, make quick connections with specially made parts, and, because of its flexibility, lay it in curves to follow your planting patterns. For simple basin irrigation, use ½-inch plastic tubing.

A system of rigid plastic pipe could be buried beneath a few inches of soil (so long as openings for water emission are above ground). The flexible plastic tubing was designed to rest on the soil surface, but it can easily be obscured by mulch. Wherever winter temperatures fall low enough to freeze water in the pipes, you must be sure to drain systems completely in the fall.

Mulching to conserve water

Hand in hand with watering comes the subject of mulches and mulching, for mulches are as effective as a cloudy day in conserving water you have given to the plants.

In addition to being practical, most mulches will put the finishing touch on the appearance of your rose garden: the wall-to-wall carpeting beneath the bushes.

Basically, a mulch is any material which you put on top of the soil to retard moisture loss and to keep soil cool. You can use a tremendous variety of materials—from organics (such as animal manures) to inorganic ones like stones. Whatever you choose, its primary function is to retard evaporation from soil so that roots do not experience rapid and severe alternations between wet and dry, cool and hot. And this is the other immediate benefit of a mulch: it keeps soil cool, simply by putting a barrier between the sun's warming rays and the ground surface. Feeder roots close to the surface benefit greatly from this moderation. For this reason, however, rose growers in regions where soil temperature remains below freezing during much of the winter usually prefer to delay mulching until the soil has warmed up from its winter chill. Applying a mulch as soon as spring arrives may slow root growth by keeping soil too cool.

Generally, a mulch an inch or two thick also will turn out to be an effective weed control agent, particularly if the ground has been weeded thoroughly sometime before laying the mulch. Any weed seeds that germinate in the mulch can be pulled from it easily.

Any organic mulch will eventually decompose

(some quickly, some over a period of years), and this process produces their final benefit. For in decomposing they constantly improve the structure of the upper soil zone, making it more open and therefore more receptive to water and air penetration and easier for the growth of feeder roots.

What mulches to use. Before you select a material for mulching, you need to know how that material acts when spread out in a layer and how fast it decomposes. The fast decomposing ones (manures, sawdust or wood shavings, compost, and lawn clippings, for example) will help improve the surface soil most quickly. But some of these—notably wood by-products (unless they are nitrogen fortified)—will take nitrogen from the soil to aid their decomposition; unless nitrogen is plentiful enough for both mulch and roses, your roses will suffer a deficiency. A *light* sprinkling of a high-nitrogen fertilizer should stave off any problem of competition for nitrogen. Manures, of course, are the classic example of a relatively quick-to-decompose material that contains enough nitrogen for its own breakdown.

Some materials, such as lawn clippings and some leaves, mat down so tightly that they prevent air and water from entering the soil. You can use lawn clippings, however, if you apply them in a thin layer and let that dry before adding fresh ones.

Cocoa bean hulls and other hard, crushed materials may be with you for several years but do the least toward improving soil structures. Rock mulches and ground covers absorb great amounts of heat and radiate it up underneath the foliage. This amounts to a hotfoot where summers are warm and dry.

Probably the trickiest material to use as a mulch—and therefore one to avoid—is peat moss. It dries out quickly after the original wetting and, if allowed to dry completely, becomes almost waterproof.

There are countless regionally available "waste" materials that you could use for mulching. In addition to manures and wood by-products, you might encounter crushed sugar cane residue *(bagasse)*, cotton seed hulls, ground corn cobs, spent mushroom compost from mushroom farms, apple or grape pomace, pine needles, or decomposed materials from the floor of forests or woods.

When applying any mulch, don't pile it up on the base of the canes; spread it to within about an inch of the base of each rose.

FERTILIZING

If a rose bush isn't fertilized, it won't necessarily wither away. In fact, many species and shrub roses can flourish reasonably well without any assistance from the plant pantry of nutrients. The public fancy, though, has fastened on the streamlined beauty of the hybrid tea or the opulence of a hybrid perpetual, not the simpler charm of the more self-sufficient wildlings. And these modern beauties *do* need fertilizer in order to dazzle us with bloom. Along with beautiful flowers and foliage, additional benefits come from a sensible fertilization program. A rose in vigorous good health is better able to withstand invasions of insects or diseases than is the one struggling for survival; and where winters are severe, the plant that has been healthy all year is more likely than the weakling to cope successfully with winter cold.

What are the major nutrients?

Like most familiar plants, roses require principally three nutrients for healthy growth: nitrogen, phosphorus, and potassium. All garden soils contain these nutrients in varied quantities. But because plants continually are at work diminishing the supply, sooner or later the gardener must begin to replenish the soil's reserves. The reasons for the importance of nutrients to roses are discussed in the following paragraphs.

• *Nitrogen* controls the rate and quantity of growth by regulating a plant's ability to make proteins, the growth promoters contained in each plant cell. When roses receive enough nitrogen, they produce an abundance of canes, stems, and leaves. If you apply too much, though, you simply overstimulate vegetative production at the expense of flowers, possibly ending up with lush foliage that lacks disease resistance, and weak, spindly growth that can be damaged easily by cold. (Or, you may find yourself with a dead plant—a casualty of fertilizer-burned roots.) Roses that are just sitting still or are only halfheartedly performing may need the stimulating tonic of a nitrogenous fertilizer. No other nutrient so rapidly improves growth when properly applied (see page 77), as long as plants are receiving adequate water. Nitrogen's effects are shown quickly in an increased volume of growth, more intense green color, greater leaf size, and more and better blooms.

A gas in its elemental form, nitrogen is available to plants only from the compounds it forms with other elements, and then it is usable largely in its nitrate form. (Nitrogen in its ammonia or nitrite forms usually is converted by soil microorganisms into nitrate to be used by plants.) Another peculiarity of nitrogen is that it is readily water soluble in most of its compounds. Unlike the other nutrients, nitrogen is not easy to stockpile in the soil because of this solubility. Much of the nitrogen not taken up by the rose soon after application will be leached out of the root zone by routine deep waterings and rain, especially in sandy soil.

• *Phosphorus* may be thought of as a regulator of the plant's seasonal life cycle. When soils contain enough available phosphorus compounds, root development begins early in the season, permitting early assimilation of other nutrients. Flower formation also is encouraged, for phosphorus plays a vital role in seed production and, later on, the maturity of the plant's growth. Plants need phosphorus for production of sugars, and it provides the mechanism by which energy released by the burning of these sugars is transferred within the plant. In definitely acid soils, phosphorus may be plentiful but will be in insoluble compounds; raising your soil's pH to the range suitable for roses (see "Soil Testing," page 76) will release much of this locked-up reserve. When other nutrients are available, a phosphorus deficiency alone may show as stunted growth with fewer flowers than normal. Because so little phosphorus is lost through leaching, it is best applied at planting time in the soil at the bottom of the planting hole.

• *Potassium* is the third member of the vital trio. Like nitrogen and phosphorus, it is not available to plants in its elemental form but always through the compound potassium oxide (K_2O), usually referred to as "potash." As an important "body builder" of plants, potassium contributes to the manufacture and movement of sugars, starches, and cellulose. It promotes the growth of strong canes and builds resistance to low temperatures.

You are less likely to encounter a potassium deficiency than a low level of nitrogen or phosphorus. Clay soils and the heavier loams generally contain enough; it is in lighter, sandier soils or in highly organic "peat" soils that potassium is more likely to be low.

Secondary and trace nutrients

Only because plants need calcium, magnesium, and sulfur in far smaller amounts than they do the "big three" (nitrogen, phosphorus, and potassium), are these nutrients called "secondary." But, a short supply of any one of these second-string nutrients can affect your roses as negatively as a lack of any of the main team.

Calcium aids in the manufacture and growth of plant cells and in root system growth. Magnesium is an important component of chlorophyll, the green material in the leaves that is necessary for photosynthesis to occur. Sulfur, like nitrogen, contributes to the formation of plant proteins.

Seven other nutrients in the soil—boron, chlorine, copper, iron, manganese, molybdenum, and zinc—provide essential elements for proper plant development, but each is needed only in very small quantities. An iron deficiency called *chlorosis* probably is the most frequently encountered trace element deficiency: leaves turn yellow but veins remain green. Usually the problem stems from iron in the soil being unavailable to plants rather than from its being absent. (This happens most often in alkaline soils.) In fact, you will seldom find deficiency of trace nutrients except in situations of extreme soil acidity or alkalinity (see "Soil Testing," page 76). An adjustment of pH to a range favorable to roses may be

all that is necessary to restore a trace element availability. Any addition of trace elements (other than iron) to your soil should be done with caution and preferably only after you have had your soil tested for pH and analyzed for nutrient content. An over-abundance of these trace nutrients can be as detrimental as a deficiency.

Your choice of fertilizer types

The choice is yours: whether to use a balanced fertilizer (often called a "complete" fertilizer) that contains all necessary major nutrients, or whether to apply the nutrients separately from different sources. What is important is that there be enough nutrients available in the soil solution to get your roses off to a good start and keep them going. Remember that *all* nutrients must be available to your roses for them to produce vigorous, healthy plants. A deficiency or absence of any one nutrient will show in the way your roses grow, or in the appearance of their leaves.

Gardeners speak of *organic* and *inorganic* fertilizers—terms reflecting the origins of the nutrients supplied by a particular fertilizer. In addition, fertilizers of each type can be applied in dry (as powder or pellets) or liquid form. And although most fertilizers are applied to the soil for roots to absorb, some fertilizers in solution can be sprayed on rose foliage and absorbed by the leaves. The sections that follow present the relative merits of the various fertilizer types.

Organic vs. inorganic fertilizers. Basically, you can separate the fertilizers into two main categories: organic and inorganic. Most organic fertilizers are derived from once-living organisms—plants (compost or cottonseed meal, for example) or animals (such as manures, bone meal, or blood meal). Exceptions are the pulverized rock products such as rock phosphate which, though not remains of once-living organisms, are processed from naturally occurring materials. In most cases you can count on the dry organics to be slower acting than dry inorganics because most of the organics must first be acted upon by soil microorganisms in order to release nutrients. (Manure is a notable exception; its nitrogen is simply leached out by water.)

Organic fertilizers offer several advantages. They all contribute, more or less, to the organic content of your soil and help it maintain a good structure. They are unlikely to stimulate your plants too early (or too late) in the year because the soil microorganisms that aid their conversion to usable nutrients are not active unless the soil is warm. You run less risk of applying too much fertilizer because nutrient concentrations are generally lower than those in inorganics, and because organics require the intermediate step with microorganisms.

One drawback to organic fertilizers, however, stems from this dependence on soil microorganisms for release of nutrients. As we've said, these microorganisms become active as soil warmth increases, but in much of the country, roses need their first nitrogen "push" of the growing season earlier in the year than when the microorganisms become active. The nitrogen in the organic fertilizer won't be made available to plant roots until the microorganisms have converted it into a form that roots can assimilate. Another possible disadvantage to organics may be cost per pound of actual nutrient. Pound for pound, most organic fertilizers contain a smaller quantity of a given nutrient than do many inorganics. For example, you would need about a ton of manure to supply the amount of nitrogen available in a 25-pound bag of ammonium sulfate.

The advantage of the inorganic fertilizers is that they can supply a predictable amount of nutrients and provide the needed nutrients without delay—and without any harm, if used according to directions. If they're carelessly used, however, the application can harm your plants: highly concentrated nutrient solutions reaching roots all at once may inflict considerable damage to young roots. And, of course, the gardener who relies solely upon inorganics for plant nutrition without adding organic materials to improve his soil is likely to find himself with a gradually deteriorated soil structure and, consequently, poor plant growth.

In recent years, two sorts of inorganic fertilizers have been developed to overcome some of the potential disadvantages of many inorganics. Urea (or urea-form, short for urea-formaldehyde) is a synthetically produced equivalent of the nitrogen in animal urine. Its nitrogen content is high, and so is its resistance to leaching. Inorganics also have been produced in various slow-release formulations, designed for a gradual, more lasting effect after application. These have been used with great success by rose growers. Where the growing season is short, the slow but steady nutrient release from an initial spring application may suffice for the entire season. In milder winter regions, early spring and midsummer applications have proven adequate.

Whichever fertilizer you select, remember that it should supply the necessary nutrients when the bushes need them. The first spring growth will be better served by an immediately available inorganic fertilizer in case soil microorganisms have not yet "awakened" for the year. Likewise, an early autumn application of soluble inorganic phosphorus-potash fertilizer will help to promote maturity and contribute to the plants' abilities to withstand winter cold where this is a problem. During the growing season, however, the choice is wide open.

Dry vs. liquid fertilizers. In the discussion of organic versus inorganic fertilizers, emphasis was on the dry fertilizer that you apply to the soil surface and water in. Periodic watering gradually dissolves the fertilizer, carrying the nutrients in solution to the roses'

roots. Such fertilizers, whether organic or inorganic, are the most widely used because they are easy to apply and because they will release their nutrients over a period of time. This minimizes the number of times each year you will need to apply fertilizer.

Liquid fertilizers, too, are justifiably popular among many rose growers. Because the nutrients are applied in a water solution, the roots will absorb the nutrients immediately, often producing a response so quickly that you almost can see it happen. You can select from an extensive array of brands and formulas, either in liquid or powder form, to be mixed with water before application.

If you grow only a few bushes, you may be content to mix the solution in a watering can and go from bush to bush with it, mixing more solution as often as needed. However, for a large rose garden you'll probably want to make a small investment in a siphon hose attachment. With this you mix a bucketful of concentrated fertilizer solution. The water flowing through the hose extracts a measured amount of this fertilizer through the siphon and dilutes it to the proper strength in the water that comes out of the hose.

Liquids are a great shot in the arm for neglected bushes and are a fine supplement to a dry fertilizer

Soil Testing

If you are doing all the "right" things for your roses but their performance doesn't measure up to your expectations, or if you just want to eliminate any guesswork from your fertilization program, have your soil tested. The most basic test will indicate your soil's acidity or alkalinity, expressed in pH numbers. A pH between 6.5 (slightly acid) and 7.2 (slightly alkaline) is considered best for roses. In this range, all necessary nutrients should be available to roots if the nutrients are present in the soil. As alkalinity or acidity increases, some nutrients become unavailable even though contained in the soil. In alkaline soils above pH 7.2, iron-deficiency chlorosis is the most commonly seen problem of this type: usually the iron is there but, because of the high pH, is locked up in insoluble compounds, unavailable to plants.

You can buy soil testing kits, or you may arrange for testing by your county department of agriculture, state university, or private soil testing agencies. The professionally conducted tests can give you the most detailed analyses and may be accompanied by recommendations for how to correct any problems that are indicated. Regardless of who conducts the test, carefully follow directions for obtaining the soil sample: otherwise results may be meaningless.

program. Most rose growers have used them just as a supplement to dry fertilizers, but gardening trends point toward increased usefulness of liquids as a regular and even total nutrient source. Roses grown in containers require individual watering attention, and it is little extra trouble to add liquid fertilizer to a watering can full of plain water. For fertilizing a number of container specimens, you can add fertilizer to the water flowing from the hose via the siphon device previously mentioned. Or you can add fertilizer through a hose-end proportioner that holds fertilizer concentrate in a glass jar and, controlled by an adjustable dial, effects the proper fertilizer dilution at the hose end. For roses grown in the ground and watered by a drip or trickle irrigation system (see pages 72–73), you can use the siphon attachment previously described to inject fertilizer into the irrigation system.

Foliar fertilizing. Since your roses can assimilate nutrients in two ways—through their roots and through their leaves—spraying fertilizer solutions onto foliage can be a beneficial *supplement* to soil fertilization. And it is simple to fertilize roses through their leaves. Just spray the nutrient solution on the foliage as you would an insecticide. The nutrient solution is taken into the leaves through the breathing pores (stomates) on their undersides and is available almost immediately for the plant's use. Many foliar fertilizers can be mixed with some of the common insecticides and fungicides so that one trip around the garden can accomplish several objectives. But don't guess—be sure all are compatible. Check labels for any warnings; if you have any questions, check with your County Cooperative Extension Advisor (or agricultural advisor) or with a successful rose grower in your area.

Foliar fertilization is no miracle worker, but it can be very helpful used in conjunction with regular soil fertilizers, leading to these possible improvements in your roses: more strong canes originating from the lower portions of your bushes, larger and darker green leaves, and more flowers.

Because more of the fertilizer is absorbed on the undersides of leaves, be sure you direct the spray there; upper surfaces will be covered by the "rain back" from this spray. Add a "spreader-sticker" to the solution to insure the spray's adhering to the leaves (or use a phosphate-free household dishwashing detergent—about ¼ teaspoon to a gallon of solution—adding the detergent after the fertilizer solution has been mixed).

If you decide to try foliar fertilization, be sure to use a fertilizer that is made for this purpose and follow label directions exactly. Too concentrated a solution is almost sure to cause some leaf burn. A consistent program is best if you expect to reap the full rewards of this method. Begin in spring when the first leaves have formed and continue every 2 to 3 weeks until midsummer in cold-winter regions or until about mid-September where winters are mild. One word of

caution: foliar fertilizing also may cause leaf burn in hot weather. As a rule-of-thumb, if temperature is 90°F/32°C or above, don't foliar fertilize.

How to select and apply fertilizers

You can feed your roses some of the major and secondary nutrients separately. But many rose growers, both new and old hands, prefer the convenience of a good, balanced, commercial fertilizer. In these fertilizers the major nutrients (and sometimes the secondary ones) are blended in specific proportions, guaranteeing a uniform relationship between the nutrients. Some of these balanced fertilizers, marketed as "rose food," have nutrients in proportions that will suit most rose growing conditions throughout the country. For the new rose grower, this is the easiest sort of fertilizer to use. Some even contain systemic insecticides that remain effective in the plant for about a month and can kill sucking insects during that time.

Usually, on the front of the packages of these "complete" fertilizers you will find three numbers, for example: 1–2–3. These numbers indicate the proportions of the three major nutrients: nitrogen, phosphorus, and potassium, in that order. (Translation: the fertilizer contains 1 percent nitrogen, 2 percent phosphoric acid, and 3 percent potash.) These percentages will be listed, beginning with nitrogen, on the back of the package, as will percentages of any other nutrients in the fertilizer.

With any of these fertilizers, *carefully* follow directions and dosage instructions on the package. Don't think that if a little fertilizer is good, more will be better: this can do more harm than good. If you are tempted to deviate from the recommendations, use *less* at a time and make the applications more often.

Before you apply dry commercial fertilizers, be sure the soil is moist to avoid burning roots. The simplest insurance is to water your roses the day before you plan to fertilize. On the next day, *lightly* scratch up the soil surface (no more than about ½-inch deep) and scatter the directed amount of fertilizer beneath the bush out to the edge of its foliage drip line, keeping it several inches away from the base of the plant. Then—and this is most important—thoroughly soak in the fertilizer.

Timing the applications. Fertilize first in early spring soon after you finish pruning. Regarding further applications, there are at least two schools of thought. One "school" says that fertilizers should be synchronized with your roses' blooming periods so that plants will receive the nutrients when they need them most: just after they have completed one burst of bloom and need to make new growth for the next. This has been called, by at least one eminent rosarian, the "pat-on-the-back" method of fertilization. If you want to break it down to numbers and enter it on the calendar, you can figure that, on the average, the cycle of growth from the start of a flowering shoot to the opening of a bud covers 45 to 60 days.

The second fertilization theory might be called the "kick-in-the-pants" method. Following this, you fertilize in smaller, but regular, doses, 2, 3, or 4 weeks apart. Those who fertilize every 2 weeks usually alternate a dry fertilizer with a liquid soil or foliar fertilizer. This theory holds that because nutrient need is continuous and because nitrogen, especially, may be so easily leached from the soil, one heavy application every 6 weeks may not continue to provide enough for a plant during that entire period.

Actually, both approaches can work very well. The "pat-on-the-back" method is easier simply because you fertilize less often; but if that is your choice, you will want to stick to the powdered or pelletized dry fertilizers that release their nutrients over a period of time. Gardeners with fast-draining soils usually find they get better results from the more frequent method.

Even if you use a timed-release fertilizer that will provide nutrients over half or more of the growing season, you may wish to give your roses additional nutrient boosts while they are actively growing. For this, a liquid fertilizer (see page 76), applied either to foliage or soil, will provide supplementary nutrition in amounts that you can regulate easily.

When to stop. Rose growers in regions where winter temperatures dip below about 10°F/−12°C have to consider when to *stop* fertilizing. Succulent new growth late in the season is likely to be ruined by fall frosts, and the plant that is still actively growing when freezing weather arrives is at a real disadvantage in getting through winter with little damage. Depending on how early the first damaging frost usually is expected, cold-climate rosarians give their last nitrogen applications anywhere from August 1 to early September—or no later than 6 weeks before anticipated freezing. Among many rose growers in these regions it is common practice to apply a phosphorus and potash fertilizer (say, 0–20–20 formula) a month to 6 weeks before frosts arrive in order to bring canes to maturity.

COMMON SENSE PEST CONTROL

Probably more potential rose enthusiasts have had their ardor dampened by long lists of pests and the measures to control them than by any other aspect of rose culture. Too often the rose has been characterized as a tender, desirable princess constantly endangered by the twin dragons of insects and disease. Though roses are attractive to various insects and some diseases, much of the formidable-sounding pest control advice that has filtered down to the rose-growing public has been geared toward rosarians who are also avid exhibitors at rose shows. To compete in shows, a rose flower, plus its stem and foliage, should be absolutely unblemished; but for the average gardener, an imperfect or chewed leaf here and there won't diminish the roses' beauty or the gardener's enjoyment of them.

In the phrase "pest control," the key word is *control*. Rather than aim for the antiseptic garden through pest elimination, the experienced gardener tries to limit potential pests and diseases to levels where plant damage will be minimal. The first step toward such control is to learn how a pest or disease affects the plant and at what time of year it is most likely to appear. Some pests can be controlled by simply washing the foliage where they appear with a forceful spray of water. This saves not only the expense of chemical remedies but also avoids needless killing of harmless or beneficial insects. Knowledge of a pest or disease's life cycle and period of usual occurrence will enable you to evaluate how minor or serious its appearance on your roses might be.

Keep your plants healthy

A healthy plant is your first line of defense against pests and diseases. Constant application of chemical sprays won't turn a sickly rose into a healthy one if it has had to endure poor soil, insufficient water, lack of nutrients, a poor garden location, or unfavorable climate.

Every year, your first effort toward establishing basic garden health should be a good spring cleaning (although in mild regions you'll do it in winter). Right after you prune your roses, clean up all leaves and other debris on the ground beneath the bushes and, before new growth emerges, give both plants and soil a thorough dormant spray (see "Pruning aftercare," page 84, for spray suggestions). This application should kill most insect eggs and disease spores that have overwintered on soil, old leaves, or rose canes.

As the season progresses, your decision to employ any pest or disease control measures will depend on your observations. And since you will be enjoying your roses almost daily, early detection will be easy. In time you will develop your own routine to handle whatever insects or diseases you find routinely visit your roses.

Basics of control

The following points, basic to whatever pest control you might employ, will help you to keep your efforts to an effective minimum.
• Insects and diseases come in cycles according to season and weather. It is senseless to employ remedies before a problem appears (certain foliage diseases excepted), or to continue using control methods after weather conditions that favor the problem have gone. Both pests and diseases are most prevalent during the warmest part of the year.

- If you have a choice of several materials to control a particular problem, choose the least toxic one for trial.
- If a chemical control for an insect pest is needed, check to see if one of the systemic insecticides (see page 80) would be effective. (A systemic is absorbed into the plant so that for a period of time following application any sucking insect that ingests the plants' juices will be killed.) For susceptible insects, one application of systemic spray may take the place of several contact spray applications.
- For nearly all pests and diseases, just one application of a contact spray or a nontoxic control (see page 80) is usually ineffective in solving the problem. A follow-up, generally within a week to 10 days, will be needed to catch newly hatched eggs or spores that the first treatment did not touch.
- Carefully read all directions on a spray label before you mix and use the materials and follow the directions exactly. If you have any reason to deviate from the directions or if you are unsure of what controls will combine safely, always seek advice before experimenting. Check with your County Cooperative Extension Advisor (or agricultural advisor), or seek the advice of a successful rose grower in your area.
- Many of the current insecticides are compatible with the standard fungicides, so if you need to control both pests and diseases, you may be able to do both with one spray solution. But remember to check product labels carefully for any compatibility cautions before you mix more than one chemical in solution. Some foliar fertilizers may be combined with insect and disease control chemicals. With these you can control and fertilize in one operation. But again, check carefully for compatibility warnings.

To spray or to dust

For routine pest control operations, you have a choice of spraying or dusting. Neither approach is categorically better than the other; the one you choose depends upon personal preference, climatic conditions, how many roses you may have to cover—and, ultimately, how well the approach works for you.

Dusting. An older form of control, it is easier in one respect: you do no mixing—just put the dust from its package into an applicator and go to work. And when you're finished, there's no need to clean out the duster.

Coverage by dusts is generally not quite as thorough as coverage by sprays, but they may be longer lasting. Although some people object to the appearance of dust residue on leaves, it is this residue that tends to make dusts a little longer lasting (provided it does not rain) than sprays. In areas where air pollution is frequent, dusts further hamper the leaves' ability to transpire; sprays, with their washing action, are preferable there.

Although duster designs vary (as do the principles by which they work), they all fall into one of two categories—continuous or intermittent flow. The continuous flow sorts are the best (and the least tiring) to use on large or medium-sized gardens. For the modest rose garden or just a few plants, one of the intermittent action types, bellows or plunger-operated, will do the job nicely, and allow you a little better control of coverage since you determine when the duster will emit its powder. Such dusters also are excellent for small touch-up applications. In fact, you can keep one loaded and ready to go at a moment's notice. Any duster should have a deflecting nozzle so that you can reach the leaves' undersides easily.

Do your dusting when the air is still, for even the slightest breeze tends to blow the dust everywhere but on the roses. Early mornings and evenings usually are the best times to dust. And don't leave your roses looking as if you had dumped sacks of flour on them; a light, relatively inconspicuous coating is enough.

Spraying. Of the several points in its favor, perhaps the most important is the wide variety of materials available for you to use. In addition to water, contact sprays, and briefly residual ones, you also have at your disposal systemic insecticides and fungicides. And with a really fine spray mist, you can penetrate more deeply into the cracks and crevices of leaves and flowers than you can with dusts.

The kind of sprayer you choose will be determined largely by the number of bushes you have. With 100 bushes and a 1-gallon sprayer you'd spend almost as much time filling the sprayer as you'd spend on spraying the bushes. You're much more likely to spray as often as necessary if you can make one solution and finish the garden with it. No matter what type you choose, however, it should be designed for easy coverage of the undersides of leaves.

Least expensive and simplest to prepare is the hose-attachment sprayer, a bottle and siphon arrangement that you attach as a nozzle to a garden hose which operates it by water pressure. You measure liquid spray concentrate into the bottle and dilute it with water according to instructions on the spray label. This solution is metered through a needle valve into the hose stream, where it is diluted to the proper concentration as it is discharged through a nozzle on the bottle cap. Offsetting ease of use, however, are several disadvantages to the hose-attachment sprayer. These applicators are more wasteful of spray solution than are the other sprayers mentioned below. Consequently, they discharge greater quantities of toxic materials than are necessary for control. With these sprayers it is difficult to cover the undersides of leaves, especially those low on the plant; and if you fail to clean the siphon part after each spraying, the sprayer's efficiency may be impaired by a buildup of spray residue—resulting in improper dilution of spray material.

Compressed-air tank sprayers are available in capacities of 1 to 6 gallons, so they are suitable for both small and fairly large gardens. With these sprayers, the spray concentrate is measured into the tank and diluted with the required amount of water. Then you close the tank top and pump a plunger to get a high pressure for good coverage. Frequently agitate the tank while you are spraying to keep the solution mixed.

The drawbacks of the larger tanks are their weight and cumbersomeness when loaded. Unless weight-lifting is your forte, look for the larger models that have a wheel attachment. For freedom of movement among your roses, be sure to get one with the longest possible hose, at the end of which is a tube with a 45° angle just before the spray head. This allows for easy spraying under the leaves.

If you are a really ambitious rose grower with 200 or more plants to spray, you may find a gasoline or electric-powered tank sprayer a necessity. Operating at a maintained hose pressure of over 100 pounds, these tanks can throw a finely atomized spray with great force over a considerable area—actually giving greater coverage with less material than other sprayers deliver. With one of these you could cover about 500 large bushes in 2 hours without having to make any additional dilutions after your initial mixing. Sizes range from 10 gallons on up; tanks usually are mounted on wheels for easy movement.

How to spray or apply the material so it can do the most good is as important as choosing the right control materials and an efficient applicator. The following five points should be observed whenever you employ a toxic pest control material.

● Thoroughly cover both sides of the leaves. Begin at the base of each bush and work upward with a side-to-side rolling movement of the spray nozzle. Your objective is to cover the underside of every leaf, for this is the region most attractive to insects and disease. By the time you reach the top of the bushes, most of the upper leaf surfaces will have been covered, too, by the "rainback" of your spray. If not, a quick spray over the tops should finish the job. Manufactured spreader-stickers, when added to a spray solution, will increase a spray's effectiveness by making it coat the leaves and adhere to them better. Even household detergent added to the spray solution (up to ¼ teaspoon to a gallon of spray) will help.

● Spray early in the morning but after most of the dew has left the plants, or in early evening after the sun's heat has decreased. This avoids the possibility of sunburn on wet leaves. To lessen the chance of leaf burn after spraying, tap or gently shake the bushes to rid them of surplus spray drops. To avoid fostering foliage diseases, you want dry foliage by nightfall. In a humid-summer climate, morning spraying is the safest.

● Do your spraying on a day following a thorough watering of the plants to be sprayed. A well-watered plant is less susceptible to chemical burn to its foliage than is a bush in need of water.

● Be very careful of the drift of your sprays and dusts.

Many garden chemicals that are relatively safe around human beings are toxic to wildlife—especially to fish. Cover nearby fishponds and bird baths while you spray, and don't dump excess spray or wash out spray equipment where it could get into ponds or streams.

● Thoroughly clean out your sprayer after each job. This will keep your sprayer in best working order and prolong its life.

PLANT PROBLEMS AND THEIR REMEDIES

Insect pests and foliage diseases that may visit your roses are illustrated and described below. Following each description is a list of possible remedies presented in three categories.

Nontoxic: control is achieved by means other than a chemical poison.

Contact: the chemical control kills the insect or disease by surface contact.

Systemic: the toxic ingredient is absorbed into the plant so that for a period of time following application any sucking insect that ingests the plant's juices will be killed.

It should be stressed that the following are only *potential* problems. Just because they *can* bother roses does not mean that your rose garden will be troubled by any or all of them, or that those that do appear will be significant enough to warrant control measures.

Insects

Numerous insecticides are available for the destruction of just about anything that crawls onto your rose plant to sample it. Many of these, however, can be very hazardous to other living things. The best policy is to determine what insect (or pests) are bothering your roses, then choose the least toxic control possible for your spray. Remember that many pests have natural enemies that could help you as long as you don't eliminate them, too, from your garden.

 **Aphids** are found nearly everywhere and on a tremendous variety of garden plants. Green, red, brown, or black—they are all soft-bodied, about ⅛ inch long. In very early spring they make their debut on tender new growth; if they congregate in great numbers and are not eradicated they may deform this growth, generally slowing or stunting development. Fortunately, aphids are the easiest pest to eliminate.

Nontoxic: water wash, spray with soap solution

Contact: diazinon, malathion, nicotine sulfate, pyrethrins
Systemic: cygon, disyston, meta-systox-R, orthene

Mites—spider mites, red spider, two-spotted mites—whatever you call them their damage is the same: they cause yellowed, dry-looking leaves, sometimes with silvery white webbing underneath. These are a warm weather pest, and the hotter the temperature the more rapidly they develop from egg to adult and the more eggs they lay. Therefore, early control is essential.

Mites do their damage by sucking the cell sap from surface tissues of leaves, causing them to change to a yellow or bronze color; the underside then turns pale brown speckled with white dots and webbing. If the mite invasion remains unchecked, the leaves will drop off, and in time an entire plant may be defoliated.

Although mites are so small you barely can see them on a rose leaf, you can check for them in two simple ways. Hold a piece of white paper beneath a suspected leaf and tap the leaf; any mites will fall onto the paper, where you'll be able to see them as little specks vainly scurrying for cover. Or, if you have a magnifying glass, use this to check the undersides of leaves. Lower leaves usually are the first to be affected.

The simplest way to combat mites is with your garden hose and water. Use a nozzle that will give you a fine spray of water, and thoroughly wash off the undersides of your rose leaves. Done several days in succession, this will disrupt their breeding and hatching cycle—and may eliminate the population. It is important that you do this at least three times—3 days in a row or *every other day*—because you need to get the mites that will hatch from eggs that already were laid when you began this hosing-off program.

Agricultural chemists have developed special formulations for mite eradication. You can either buy these separately or use a general purpose spray that contains both insecticides and fungicides. For a really effective mite cleanup, be sure to spray at least twice or preferably three times, waiting 5 days between sprayings. Thoroughly drench the *undersides* of the leaves: that's where the mites are. The first shot kills adult mites, the second should get new ones hatching from eggs that existed at the time you first sprayed and before they mature and lay additional eggs. It is virtually impossible, though, to be 100 percent effective each time, and only a few leftovers can cause a new infestation. So it is definitely to your advantage to spray a third time.

Spider mites rather quickly become immune to any one insecticide. If you spray for mites throughout a season, change miticides after several applications.

Nontoxic: water wash
Contact: kelthane, plictran
Systemic: none

Thrips can be the most discouraging pests because their chief target is flowers. Special favorites of theirs are white, yellow, and other light-colored varieties. Small as they are (about 1/20 inch long), their rasping and puncturing of petal surfaces can cause considerable discoloration and disfiguration. Thrips attack buds in their early stages, working among the unfolded petals. In severe cases, buds become deformed and fail to open properly, while the damaged petals turn brown and dry. New growth also may be damaged in the same way.

A light misting of buds and blooms twice a week with a specific thrips insecticide during a heavy infestation usually will give good control.

Nontoxic: none
Contact: diazinon, malathion
Systemic: cygon, meta-systox-R, orthene

Beetles of various kinds may sample your roses' leaves and flowers. The damage they do may be so slight that it can be tolerated, or their numbers so few that hand picking will be effective. Japanese beetles, however, can be a special problem in regions where they are prevalent; best advice for their control will come from your County Cooperative Extension Advisor (or agricultural advisor).

Nontoxic: hand pick
Contact: diazinon, sevin
Systemic: none

Caterpillars and worms collectively include the various wormlike pests that chew holes in flower buds and leaves or skeletonize leaves. Damage varies from casual to severe, and the extent of it determines the remedy.

Nontoxic: handpick, *Bacillus thuringiensis* (harmful only to the caterpillar)
Contact: diazinon, sevin
Systemic: none.

Rose midge is a near-microscopic (about 1/25 inch long) insect that does its damage in the larva stage. Eggs are deposited in the tips of new growth, usually following the first bloom cycle. The eggs hatch in a few days, and the larvae rasp the tender plant tissues causing them to blacken and shrivel. Unchecked, a heavy midge infestation can eliminate all bloom from late spring through early fall. From stem tips the larvae drop to the soil where they pupate and emerge as adult winged insects in about a week. The critical place of control is the soil; adults must be killed as they emerge. Diazinon is most effective, either in granule form sprinkled on the soil beneath roses and for a distance of at least 6 feet beyond, or in spray form applied to the same area. Follow-up applications may be needed if damage resumes later in the season.

Nontoxic: none
Contact: diazinon
Systemic: none

 **Borers** generally are responsible for the sudden wilt and droop of succulent new growth tips. Inside the shoot you will find a "worm" busily consuming the stem's pith. The only control is to cut off the damaged shoot below the damage and just above a leaf.

Nontoxic: hand pick
Contact: none
Systemic: none

Diseases

Although blackspot, powdery mildew, and rust comprise the "big three" of rose diseases, most rose growers will have to contend with only a "devilish duo." Mildew is found nationwide, but rust and blackspot territories seldom overlap. Planting your roses so that there will be a chance for air circulation around each plant will help minimize foliage disease problems. Roses growing in a single row along a driveway, for example, often will be healthier (other conditions being equal) than the same ones closely planted in a formal garden.

 **Blackspot** is definitely the most devastating of the foliage diseases. Unchecked, it can defoliate a plant at the height of the growing season. Such bushes fail to make normal growth in that year and are much more susceptible to winter damage because plants fail to mature naturally—they continually try to produce new growth to replace lost foliage.

California and the warm, semi-arid regions of the Southwest seldom encounter blackspot. Where summer rainfall is common, you find conditions that favor its spread and development: wet leaves, warmth, and splashing water to spread the infection.

The disease is well named. Black spots with irregular, fringed margins appear on the leaves and sometimes on stems. Around the spots, leaf tissue may turn yellow. With especially susceptible varieties and in severe cases, the entire leaf may yellow and drop off.

Blackspot spores live through the winter in lesions on canes and possibly on old leaves fallen to the ground. In spring they germinate and reach new foliage in splashing water from rain or overhead sprinkling. From these infections develop the characteristic spots that then produce great numbers of fresh spores to extend the infection.

Garden sanitation is your first line of defense against the fungus. Keep a watchful eye during the season.

Nontoxic: none
Contact: folpet, maneb
Systemic: funginex

In addition to funginex alone, two spray combinations can be used to combat blackspot and mildew. With folpet plus benomyl, you will have longer residual action, but foliage will burn when temperatures exceed 90°F. Maneb plus benomyl is safer in hot weather.

 **Powdery mildew** is a fungus found virtually everywhere roses are grown. Flourishing during times of high humidity but not rainy weather, it is a gray to white, furry or powdery growth that attacks new growth of leaves, stems, and flower buds. Infected leaves quickly become crumpled and distorted and will remain that way even after you kill the fungus. Damage is possible—but less severe—on mature leaves. Resistance to it varies from one variety to the next.

In contrast to blackspot which spreads in water, mildew is encouraged by a humid atmosphere but needs dry leaves to establish itself. Foggy coastal areas are ideal for its spread. Overcrowded plantings in damp and shady gardens are subject to more severe attacks than are roses in sunny beds where they have free air circulation through and between plants. Unmulched but well-watered roses will be living in a more humid atmosphere than plants with a mulch over the moist soil.

Nontoxic: water wash
Contact: acti-dione PM, folpet
Systemic: funginex, benomyl

See note under "Blackspot" for combination sprays effective against both blackspot and mildew.

 **Rust.** While the rest of the country is looking for black spots, western and southwestern rosarians are seeing red—or, more precisely, rusty-orange spots. Rust usually appears first in late spring on leaf undersides.

Small orange spots enlarge into thick, powdery masses of orange spores as yellow blotches appear on the leaf surface. Easily shaken loose by air currents and rain, they germinate quickly on damp leaves to set up new colonies of infection. In severe and unchecked cases, rust, like blackspot, can defoliate roses.

Here again, garden sanitation goes far toward reducing the incidence of disease. It is very important that you remove all old leaves from plants as well as from the ground at pruning time, especially in regions where roses never go so dormant as to lose all foliage.

During the growing season, any of the materials listed below should give adequate control. In the nearly tropical climates of Florida and Hawaii, there is no dormant season—roses grow all year, so removal of foliage is not a good idea. Gardeners there must rely entirely on foliage sprays for control.

Nontoxic: none
Contact: folpet, plantvax
Systemic: funginex

PRUNING— THEORY AND PRACTICE

Probably no other aspect of rose culture has aroused as much controversy as the subject of pruning. For well over half a century, battle lines have been drawn between the advocates of light pruning and those who champion hard cutting back. Along with a better understanding of plant physiology and rose ancestries, much trial-and-error data has been accumulated. The consensus is that light-to-moderate pruning will produce the best possible garden plants and plenty of good flowers. To understand why this is the case, let's first learn basically how a plant's roots, stems, and leaves function together, and then take a look at the history of rose pruning.

How a plant grows

The roots, stems, and leaves of a rose plant all work together for the plant's continued growth, productiveness, and increase in size. Roots, of course, not only anchor the plant in the soil, but also absorb dissolved nutrients from water present in the soil. These nutrients are then carried upward and throughout the stems of the plant in specialized cells. At the same time, leaves are taking in carbon dioxide from the atmosphere and converting it into sugars and other "foods" which can be transported throughout the plant in another type of specialized cell.

Not all absorbed nutrients and synthesized substances (such as sugars) are used immediately, however; some are stored in tissues of roots and stems to be used at some later time. Proteins, for example, are put together from glucose sugar which is produced by the leaves; they are vital to the production of new plant cells as the plant grows. These proteins can be stored in the wood and bark cells toward the end of the growing season when no appreciable new growth is being produced but while leaves still are manufacturing sugars. When growth resumes in spring, the plant draws upon this stored protein because there are no leaves to start immediately producing proteins needed for growth.

If you prune heavily, you impose several hardships on your rose plant. You have thrown away much of the plant's stored reserves (those in the stems) for starting off spring growth. This forces the plant to rely upon reserves stored in the roots for the initial growth push. And since the root system enlarges in proportion to the size of the plant—(remember, the leaves manufacture "foods" that contribute to the growth of the entire plant)—continual heavy pruning results in a small root system with correspondingly small amounts of stored nutrients to call upon in spring. Heavily pruned plants produce a more limited amount of growth at the first flush; this means fewer leaves will be there to begin manufacturing growth substances for additional new growth.

Development of rose pruning

Rose pruning, as the annual ritual we know today, grew out of the 19th-century development of varieties that have large, well-formed flowers suitable for individual exhibition at flower shows. Most of these exhibition varieties were found among the tea roses and the recently emerged hybrid perpetual class (see pages 10 and 14). To produce the really large blooms which invariably were the award winners, rose growers would severely prune their bushes every year, believing that all of the plants' energies would be concentrated into producing just a few really magnificent flowers on long stems. Plant longevity was not as important to these exhibitors as was the winning of prizes; if a good ribbon-winner proved to be "weak" in the garden, the rosarian would replace it with new plants every few years.

What was overlooked in the slavish adherence to radical pruning was a consideration of the *natural* growth habit of the roses being pruned. For simplicity, you can assume there are two growth types: those that produce new wood freely from the base and will, on their own roots, spread into large clumps; and others that tend to build up a structure of old wood and produce more new growth from old wood than from the base.

By mid-19th century, rose ancestries already were somewhat mixed, but the hybrid perpetuals tended to fall into the first group, whereas tea roses definitely fell in the second. Hybrid teas, then, inherited from their tea ancestry the inclination to build up a woody plant structure. You will notice this particularly in some varieties (such as 'Charlotte Armstrong') that tend to form a framework of canes in their first few years in the garden and then build most new growth from these canes rather than from the bud union.

Around 1900 a major hybridizing breakthrough occurred which has influenced in a dramatic way the appearance and constitution of modern hybrid teas. This was the successful introduction of the species *Rosa foetida* (through its variety 'Persian Yellow') into the new hybrid tea class (see page 14). Not only did this species carry the yellow, orange, flame, and copper shades into hybrid teas, but also it brought its dislike for *any* pruning and its tendency to die back if cut into severely. Even today, many older varieties in these colors make much better garden plants if cut back only lightly.

Modern hybrid teas, then, have inherited a distaste for regular heavy pruning. Many, of course, will endure pruning and still turn in a reasonable performance (consider parts of the country where winter cold freezes most hybrid teas down to their protective coverings), but they are more lavish with good bloom when such drastic cutting back can be avoided. To illustrate: Some hybrid teas that occur in both bush and climbing forms have had the reputation for being "better" as climbers. This sometimes is attributed to the climbing form's increased vigor, but very often it is caused by heavier pruning of the bush form. Allowed to build on old wood, the climber becomes larger and more prolific each year; the bush, on the other hand, has to make a relatively new start every spring.

Timing and tools

When is the best time to prune roses? You'll find that for most modern roses it is toward the end of the dormant season when growth buds along the canes begin to swell. Where winter temperatures are mild, this can be as early as January. In the "ice box" regions of the northeast, central, and mountain states you won't think about it until late March or April. In general, you should do the pruning in winter or early spring but not so early that the new growth which follows will be caught by late frosts.

In areas where winter lingers and its chill trades off with spring temperatures during the transitional months of March or April, gardeners often rely upon two indicators for when to prune. Thirty days before the last expected killing frost is generally a safe time; ask your county agricultural advisor for this average date. You can also assume the time is ripe when forsythia comes into bloom.

To do the job well, you need two tools: sharp pruning shears and a pruning saw. Although the shears will take care of most of the work, you'll need the saw (a small keyhole type or coping saw) for removing larger canes and those in areas that are awkward for shears. For the cleanest cuts, use the scissor-action shears with a curved steel cutting blade. Anvil type shears (in which the cutting is done by one blade against a flat metal surface) are easy to use but even when sharp can bruise the canes.

Pruning aftercare

A thorough rose garden cleanup should be an annual routine, and the easiest time for it is directly after the final pruning. First, remove any leaves that remain on your rose plants. Then rake up and discard all old leaves, prunings, and any other debris that is on the

ground or around the bases of the bushes; insect eggs and some disease spores may be carried from one year to the next on old or dead rose leaves.

Right after cleaning the rose beds, spray the pruned bushes and the ground around them as a final hedge against insect eggs and disease spores that may have remained on the plants or the soil's surface.

Other refuges for disease spores and insect eggs are the canes of rose bushes—especially in the thickened and fissured bark of older canes and at the bases of bushes—and the soil surface of the rose beds. Many rose growers therefore apply a dormant season spray right after they prune their bushes. Lime-sulfur (calcium polysulfide) or a lime-sulfur and oil combination are the traditional dormant cleanup sprays and must be used while roses are completely dormant. Simpler to apply (and every bit as effective) during the cold of late winter or early spring is a combination insecticide-miticide-fungicide made up of sprays normally used during the growing season. Such a dormant spray can be applied safely even after new growth has begun to emerge.

How to prune hybrid teas, grandifloras, and floribundas

The objectives of pruning are simply to promote a symmetrical bush, to encourage new growth, and to remove any diseased, damaged, or dead wood. Regardless of where you live, here are a few basic pruning guidelines which should help you prune any of the popular bush roses: hybrid teas, grandifloras, and floribundas. (Additional tips for climbers and for shrub and species roses are on pages 86–87.)
• Remove all dead wood and all weak, twiggy branches. If an older cane produced nothing but weak growth, remove it at the bud union.
• Open up the center of the bush by removing all branches that cross through the center. This gives you a "vase shaped" plant (a slender or a fat vase, depending on how upright or spreading the variety grows) without a profusion of twigs and leaves in the middle where insects and diseases could hide out and flourish. Note: rosarians in very hot climates often just shorten the branches that cross through the center. These will produce enough leaves to thoroughly shield canes from the scorching sun.
• Remove up to ⅓ of the length of all growth that was new during the year. To develop really large, specimen shrubs in the mild-winter areas of the South and West, don't cut into live new growth of the past season that is much thicker than a lead pencil.

If you live where winter protection is necessary and you use a method that requires reducing the bush size to fit the protector, you almost surely will remove more than ⅓ of the past year's growth. In this case, try not to reduce the height any further in spring unless there has been winter kill below your original cuts. Whatever winter protection you may use, you'll have to cut out

Fundamentals of pruning

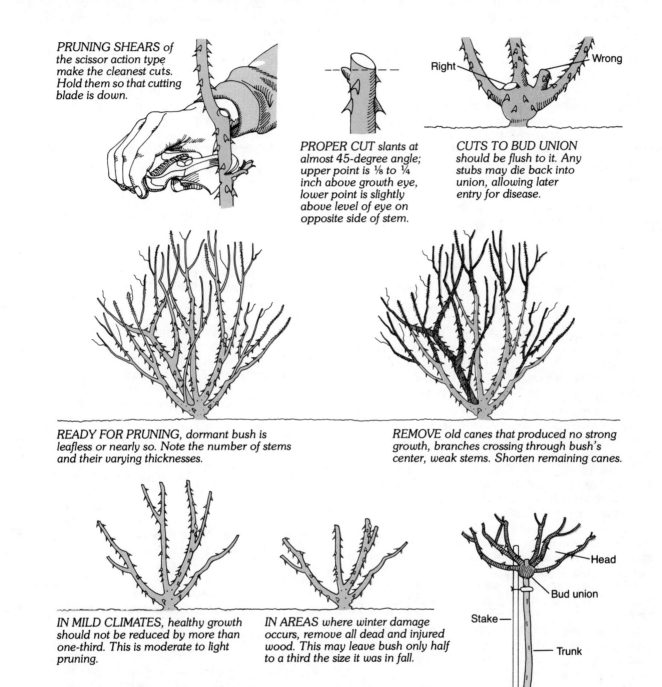

PRUNING SHEARS of the scissor action type make the cleanest cuts. Hold them so that cutting blade is down.

PROPER CUT slants at almost 45-degree angle; upper point is ⅛ to ¼ inch above growth eye, lower point is slightly above level of eye on opposite side of stem.

Right   Wrong

CUTS TO BUD UNION should be flush to it. Any stubs may die back into union, allowing later entry for disease.

READY FOR PRUNING, dormant bush is leafless or nearly so. Note the number of stems and their varying thicknesses.

REMOVE old canes that produced no strong growth, branches crossing through bush's center, weak stems. Shorten remaining canes.

IN MILD CLIMATES, healthy growth should not be reduced by more than one-third. This is moderate to light pruning.

IN AREAS where winter damage occurs, remove all dead and injured wood. This may leave bush only half to a third the size it was in fall.

Head

Bud union

Stake

Trunk

Understock

A STANDARD (popularly called "tree rose") consists of three parts: understock, stem or trunk, and head. Onto a regular understock is first budded a rose that will produce a long, thick cane for the trunk. Then a year later, the desired hybrid tea or floribunda is budded onto the trunk. Basic pruning guidelines apply to standards, with the accent on symmetry. After pruning, the head should not have any stems extending beyond its generally domed-shaped outline. Most vulnerable part of a standard is the trunk. Give each standard a sturdy stake at planting time, placing stake close to trunk and extending several inches into head. Trunks are susceptible to sun-scalding, so place stake on sunny side of trunk or wrap burlap around trunk.

all damaged wood regardless of how low this leaves your bushes. Even though a cane may be green on the outside, if the center is brown, it is damaged. Prune all stems and canes back to wood that is light green to cream-white in the center.

• Make all cuts at a 45-degree angle close above a leaf bud that points toward the outside of the plant; the lowest point should be on the side of the stem opposite the bud, but not lower than the bud itself.

• Paint all cuts larger than lead-pencil size (and particularly all cuts to the bud union) with a sealing compound. The white glue that comes in small plastic bottles with dispenser tops is easy to use and entirely satisfactory for this purpose. Just squeeze out one to several drops of glue onto the cut surface and spread it out to cover the cut. In parts of the country where rose cane borer is a problem, many rosarians cover all pruning wounds to prevent entry of borers.

How to prune climbing roses

Several distinct growth and flowering habits fall under the category of "climbing rose." What they all have in common is long, flexible canes that produce flowers from eyes along their length. For their first 2 or 3 years in your garden, your work with any of the climbers will be to train them (see page 87). Then, after their growth patterns are established and some wood has matured, you can think about how to prune them.

Climbing hybrid teas. Most climbing roses sold today can be classed as climbing hybrid teas. They bear the characteristic shapely buds throughout the entire flowering season from spring through fall. Many of these are simply climbing sports of familiar bush roses and carry the same name as the bush varieties, but preceded by the word "Climbing." The same is true for some grandifloras and floribundas.

After you plant one of these climbers, leave it unpruned for the next 2 or 3 years: it takes that long for plants to become established and produce strong climbing canes. During this period, just remove all dead canes and branches, weak growth, and spent flowers; tie new canes into position as they mature (see page 87.)

In several years' time, the plant will consist solely of long canes produced after you planted it in your garden. From these canes will come side branches (laterals) that will bear the flowers. Your pruning objectives are twofold: to encourage growth of more flowering laterals and to stimulate production of new canes to gradually replace the oldest and less productive ones. (Varieties differ in this respect; some will always throw out new canes from the base each year, whereas others build up a more woody structure and produce most long new cane growth from higher on the plant.) Therefore, don't cut back the long canes at all unless any of them are growing too long for the allotted space.

Whenever any long canes or branches grow in a direction contrary to what you want, first try to train them into place. Only if this won't work, remove them entirely (but remember—these long growths produce the flowering laterals).

For annual pruning, remove only the old and obviously unproductive wood. Then cut back to two or three eyes all of the laterals that bore flowers during the last year. The best blooms are produced on laterals growing from 2 or 3-year-old wood.

During the flowering season, just remove all spent blooms, cutting back to a strong eye two or three leaves away from the flowering shoot's point of origin.

Large-flowered climbers. These roses have just those two features in common: fairly large flowers and the climbing growth habit. Some have hybrid tealike blooms, others resemble floribundas, and a few even look like sophisticated wild roses. Some will bloom but once a year, whereas others repeat throughout summer and fall—and it is their blooming habits that are your best guide to pruning. For the first 2 or 3 years in your garden, all should receive the same treatment as recommended above for climbing hybrid teas.

Climbers that have only one flowering period should receive most of their pruning after their bloom. They flower on wood produced after their *last* year's flowering, so a dormant season pruning just throws away potential blooming wood. After they flower, cut out the least productive old canes and any weak, old, or entangling branches. New canes will grow from the base and low down on the remaining canes, and strong new laterals will grow from farther out on the older canes that you leave. From this new growth come most of the branches that will carry next year's flowers.

The large-flowered climbers that repeat their bloom throughout the year produce good flowering wood from new canes and laterals as well as from wood more than a year old. Prune these just as you would the climbing hybrid teas (see above).

With the once-blooming varieties among these natural climbers, little good is done by removing spent flowers or flower clusters. Some varieties may produce secondary blooms from the midst of old flower clusters or from just below them. Many go on to develop colorful and very decorative hips.

Pillar roses. Two sorts of climbing roses are grown as flowering pillars up to about 10 feet tall. One is the hybrid tea or floribunda climber which grows short climbing canes (about 8–10 feet long). The other is a natural pillar type which grows 6–10-foot upright canes that will flower along their length. Pruning objectives and methods are the same as for climbing hybrid teas; the principal difference is that you will train long new growth upright.

Ramblers. Each year after spring bloom, rambler roses produce many long, vigorous, and limber canes

Recognizing Sucker Growth

Any growth on a budded rose bush that comes from below the point where the named variety was budded onto the understock (see page 93) is a sucker. And all that a sucker is, really, is the understock plant trying to grow its own leaves and stems. Because a number of different understocks are in general use, no specific identifying characteristics can guide you in recognizing sucker growth. But one point is certain: the growth will be different from the rose it supports—often a long, slender, flexible cane. If you planted your roses with bud unions above soil level, you easily can see if the growth in question comes from below. For roses with bud unions at or slightly below the soil surface, carefully dig down to the growth's point of origin. If you determine you have a sucker on your hands, sharply *pull* it down and off the plant. Merely cutting it off will leave undeveloped growth eyes at the sucker's base, and they will trouble you with more suckers in the future.

from the base of the plant. Next spring's flowers come from this new growth. Flowers are typically small, but in large clusters or trusses that appear only once annually. This spring flower display, however, can be overwhelming.

Wait to prune ramblers until flowering has finished and new growth is underway. Then cut out canes that just flowered and show no sign of producing any long, vigorous new growth. As the new canes mature, train them into position.

How to train climbing roses

Climbers with canes trained horizontally or trained upward and arched over will bloom most profusely. Left to its steady upward growth, a long climbing cane will continue to build new tissues to increase only its upward growth. This is a situation known as *apical dominance*: the topmost growth continues at the expense of any lateral growth. When a long, upright cane is arched over or bent down to a horizontal position, however, the apex of growth is thwarted so that many eyes along the cane will begin to grow, each one growing upward. It is these laterals off the main canes and long branches that give you flowers.

If you have a high fence, wall, or side of a house to cover, let the vertical canes grow to about 10 feet long.

Then lean them out at an angle from the plant's base on both sides of the plant. Tie canes horizontally and space them 18 to 24 inches apart, paralleling one above the other. Arch the end of each cane downward and tie it in place. Flowering shoots will come from all along the canes. Leave as many canes as you need to achieve the desired height.

Climbers trained horizontally along a low fence or wall will tend to produce flowering shoots from most eyes in the horizontal portions of the canes. Even with horizontal canes, if you arch over about the last 12 inches (after canes have reached the desired length), bloom production will be increased.

Pruning shrub and old garden roses

The durable and venerable rose species and old varieties represent such a diversity of types and growth habits that it is difficult to generalize about them. Most, however, are vigorous growers that may need some thinning and shaping each year but very little actual cutting back. Since most of these roses are used for specimen shrubs or hedges, the primary pruning should be directed toward trimming and shaping them to fit into the landscape picture. Cut back any shoots that depart unattractively from the general pattern of the plant; remove any old canes that produced little new growth or flowers, and any weak wood.

Some old roses—especially many hybrid perpetuals—produce fairly long, arching canes in the manner of climbing roses. Like climbers, these roses produce more bloom if the canes are trained horizontally or arched over and the tips "pegged" to the ground. Then flower-producing laterals will grow from most eyes along the canes.

The shrub and old garden roses that have one flowering period per year bloom on the growth that they produced after the last year's bloom season. To prune these roses when you would your hybrid teas is to sacrifice some of their potential display. Wait until after they finish flowering; then you can cut out the least productive old wood. You also may shorten long new canes; this will encourage them to put forth more lateral growth on which the next spring's blossoms will come.

Other ways to regulate growth

After new growth is underway in early spring, check over the new shoots that are emerging to see what directions they are taking. If any appear to be poorly located or unnecessary (crossing through the center of the bush, for example) break or rub them out. By eliminating this growth you conserve the plant's energy for the strong new shoots that are well placed; you also simplify your pruning operation for the next year. Sometimes two or three new shoots will grow from one leaf axil. When you notice this, carefully rub out all but the strongest one.

During the flowering season, you will be removing flowers from your bushes—some for decoration in the house, the rest just to tidy up the plants. If you remember that the leaves are helping to provide nutrients for the plants (see page 83), you'll realize the need for leaving a good supply on the bush. When you want a few long-stemmed beauties for inside, cut each stem so that you leave *at least* two sets of leaves on the branch from which you cut the flower. Or, when you remove faded blooms from the bushes, cut down only as far as necessary to keep the bush well shaped—usually to the first 5-leaflet leaf that points away from the bush's center.

New rose bushes and weak or small plants that you're trying to build up need all possible leaves to manufacture foods. With these plants, just snap off the faded flowers, but do not cut blossoms with stems for the house.

WINTER PROTECTION

More winter injury results from sudden, rapid, or frequent temperature change than from low temperature itself. Moisture in the canes expands when it freezes, so quick freezes break cell walls inside canes and destroy vital plant tissue. Repeated alternations of freezing, thawing, and refreezing can ruin exposed canes.

Another prime factor in winter damage is desiccation. Winter winds dry out exposed canes, and if soil is frozen, roots cannot take up water to replace lost moisture. If canes have been damaged at all by cold, the injured cells can't resist water loss. In springtime you find shriveled and blackened canes in place of plump, green wood.

Many shrub and species roses can take whatever a northern winter sends their way, and some hybridizers are determinedly working to combine this hardiness with hybrid tea beauty. But until this marriage takes place, most rose growers in areas where snow falls will have to use some form of protection against the elements in order to enjoy the glories of modern hybrid teas, floribundas, and climbers.

Even among modern roses, the varieties vary considerably in hardiness. Many yellow, orange, and bronze shades are more tender than the average variety, a throwback to the yellow tea rose in their background. Hybrid perpetuals usually are more cold-tolerant than hybrid teas, and so are many of the floribundas.

Generally speaking, though, figure that all bush and climbing roses will withstand temperatures down to 10°F/−12°C unprotected. Most shrub and old garden roses can make it on their own until the temperature drops to −10°F/−23°C, and many can take much lower readings.

Tips for winter survival

Contrary to what you might expect, one purpose of winter protection is to keep roses cold, not warm. What you want are thoroughly dormant canes at a fairly constant temperature—ideally in the 15° to 25°F/−9° to −4°C range.

Actually, winter protection begins at planting time, for in areas where cold winters prevail, location and exposure can greatly influence the intensity of cold and amount of temperature fluctuation. Cold air seeks the lowest level, so valley gardens will be colder than those on surrounding hillsides. Low pockets in your garden will be consistently colder than elevated or sloping areas, and roses planted there are in danger of being frozen at the bud union unless well insulated. Plantings sheltered from wind—whether by walls, other shrubbery and trees, or your house—are likely to be warmer than exposed plantings and will suffer less from desiccation.

Often winter winds are distinctly colder than still air. In regions normally beyond their hardiness limit, climbing roses may survive winters if planted against a house or garage wall that shelters them from wind, and raises, by means of reflected heat, the overall low temperatures.

Your care during the growing season also has a great influence on potential cold tolerance. The healthy plant which grew vigorously and was not defoliated by disease or insects will stand a much better chance than the weakling which just managed to exist through the past year. Furthermore, the matured or ripened plant is not nearly as vulnerable as the one that was still actively growing and blooming when the first frosts occurred. Cells in growing stems and canes have high moisture and low starch contents; this makes them more susceptible to freezing and cell damage. In contrast, matured growth has a much higher percentage of solids in the cells than moisture. A combination of withholding nitrogen fertilizers about 6 weeks before expected frosts (page 78) and allowing September blooms to stay on the plants to form seed hips will put your roses in the well-ripened state ready to face several months of cold.

Preparation for protection

No matter what form of winter protection you decide to use, there are some basic preparations and guidelines to follow. Thoroughly clean up all old leaves and spent flowers from the rose bed and strip away any foliage that remains on canes. Left on, leaves will continue to lose moisture, and they are always a potential source of disease infection for the next year. Under rose cones, they may decay and spread disease to the canes. Be sure to remove all debris and mulch from around plant bases. Then shortly before you expect the ground to freeze, give your bushes one final deep soaking for the year.

As important as protection can be, do refrain from protecting bushes before they need it. If you mound or use cylinders, wait until you have had at least two hard freezes. Styrofoam cones shouldn't go on until the ground is frozen about 2 inches deep. Cold frame sides may go up at your convenience, but wait until you expect a 15° to 25°F/−9° to −4°C temperature before putting on the roof.

For roses protected by mounds or cylinders, you'd be wise to tie canes together with soft twine to minimize their whipping around in winter winds. For the same reason, cut back any taller than 3 feet.

Winter protection methods

MOUND SOIL at least 12 inches high over bud union of each bush (get soil from another part of garden). Cover with straw after mounds freeze, to keep mounds frozen. Cylinder of wire mesh holds mounded soil in place around canes, lets water drain away easily.

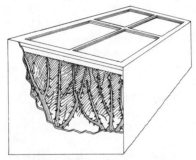

STYROFOAM ROSE CONES require canes be tied together, cut down to fit cones. Mound soil over bud union and place cone over bush; put brick on top of cone and place soil over flanges to hold cone in place.

COLD FRAME, easily made from plywood, allows protection of large bushes; hinged roof can be opened for ventilation on warm days.

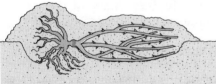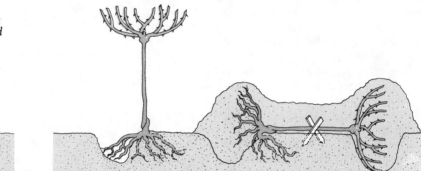

"MINNESOTA TIP," time-consuming but successful, involves digging up roots on one side of plant, bending bush over into trench, covering all with soil. To "tip" standards, bend plant over bud union of roots and trunk, pin trunk to soil, cover.

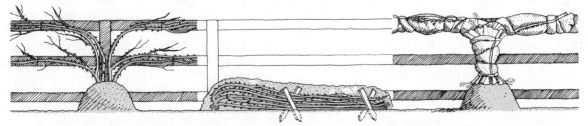

PROTECT climbing roses with soil mound where winter lows are in the +5° to +15°F/−15° to −9°C range. Cover canes with soil if lows go below −10°F/−23°C. Insulate canes with straw wrapped in burlap for −10° to +5°F/−23° to −15°C areas.

Uncovering in spring

Early springtime weather often is unpredictable. Warm days suddenly turn to freezing ones, then back to warm again any number of times before spring arrives for good. So don't be tempted by the first breath of spring to remove the roses' protection. With cold frames and removable-top rose cones, open the roof or top on warm sunny days, but close it if freezes are predicted. If your styrofoam cones have solid tops, take the entire cone off when soil thaws enough so that cones can be pulled off without breaking the flanges. Replace the cones whenever freezes are predicted.

If you use soil mounds, gradually begin to remove soil when it thaws. Do this carefully to avoid breaking any growth that may have begun under the mound.

MINIATURE ROSES

The popularity of miniature roses derives in part from their overall daintiness: they are scaled-down replicas of modern floribundas or hybrid teas in all the colors of their larger kin. A limited number are small re-creations of old garden roses — some even with "moss." Because they are so small, another reason for their popularity is obvious: they extend the joy of rose-growing to apartment dwellers with no more than a window, deck, or small patio for plants. And for rose growers with more space, they introduce a size variation to the garden; miniatures can be used as borders and small hedges, in rock-garden type plantings and in containers. There are even climbing miniatures, and some varieties are propagated as miniature standards.

Miniature is a relative term and does not mean that all miniature roses are the same dwarf size. Container culture keeps all miniatures more uniform in size, but even then the differences are apparent — some having noticeably larger flowers, leaves, and canes.

The real differences show up when miniatures are planted in the ground. Some remain a foot high or less, even under the best of conditions, while others may develop into shrubs three feet or even more in height. These large miniatures fill the same landscape niches as do floribundas — but with generally smaller flowers and finer-textured foliage. Where uniformity of size is desirable — for a hedge or a border — best results are produced by planting just one variety or by choosing varieties you've seen growing in the ground under the same conditions.

In contrast to nearly all other roses sold, bush and climbing miniatures should be grown on their own roots: even typically small plants may grow too large if budded onto understocks, thereby losing much of their diminutive charm. Miniatures are not sold bare-root either. Plants purchased locally are in small pots, and mail-order plants usually come in pots or with the root balls intact and wrapped in plastic or moist sphagnum moss. Leaves on mail-order plants may be yellowed or drooping upon arrival, but don't worry: just soak the entire plant overnight in water.

Miniatures outdoors

Soil requirements (pages 62–66) and need for sunshine are no different from other roses, but there is one important planting difference: miniatures should be set *slightly* lower than they were in their nursery containers to encourage more root formation. Distance between plants depends on ultimate size of the plants, the variety, and your climate. Remember that the milder the climate and longer the growing season, the larger the plants tend to grow.

Root systems are extensive but rather shallow, so a temporary drought imposed by a neglectful gardener is much more critical to these plants than to their larger and more deep-rooted brethren. See that soil is always moist, but not soggy. Almost certainly you'll want to use a mulch to help conserve moisture (see page 73) — and remember that a fine-textured mulch is more in keeping with the sizes of these roses.

Although miniatures are small, they still need fertilizer for best growth. But don't fertilize newly planted bushes; wait until after their first crop of bloom, then use a liquid fertilizer every 3 to 4 weeks during the rest of their first season. In their second and subsequent years in your garden, give plants a dry complete fertilizer — about 1 tablespoon per plant — at the start of the growing season, and follow up throughout the season according to suggestions on pages 74–78. The timed-release fertilizers are good for miniatures, too, supplemented by liquid fertilizer applications if need becomes apparent. Avoid fertilizers that are very high in nitrogen: they will stimulate excessive growth.

At the end of the winter dormant season, cut back plants to lowest outward facing growth eyes on previous season's stems; this leaves you with a severely pruned plant that will produce the strongest new growth for flower production. If you hesitate to prune so heavily, be sure to cut plants back by at least half, removing all weak and twiggy growth. During the growth season, remove faded blooms, cutting their stems back to about half their length. If any long, rank growth occurs, pinch or cut it back to promote branching. Pests and foliage diseases may visit miniature roses, too (see pages 78–83).

Miniatures in containers. For new bushes, an 8-inch pot is a good beginning; miniature standards may need a 10 to 12-inch pot or tub at first. Any container will be suitable as long as it provides at least a 6-inch soil depth and has drainage holes. A good container mixture contains equal parts of good garden soil, organic matter (such as peat moss), and perlite. Container-growth miniatures need careful watering. Whenever you water, be sure to give enough so that water drains out of the container; this ensures thorough watering and flushes out any potentially harmful salts that could accumulate in the potting soil.

Indoor culture

Temperature, humidity, and light are the three factors that most influence success with minatures indoors. Give plants full sunlight in a room that is 70°–75°F/ 21°–24°C during the day, and about 10°F/5°C cooler at night. Place them near a window with good light, but not direct hot sunlight. Don't put plants on a narrow window sill; the sun through the glass may burn them, and the night air could chill them. The dry atmosphere of the average home is too arid for their liking. To provide more humidity around plants, set pots on trays of gravel and fill the tray with water up to the containers' bases: the evaporating water will humidify the surrounding air. Always keep plants away from heaters. Fluorescent lights, particularly those designed for indoor plant growth, can provide adequate indoor light for miniature roses if you have no well-lighted window space. For best performance, suspend two tubes with a reflector 10 to 14 inches above the plants.

Give indoor miniature roses liquid fertilizer every three weeks to a month. Again, avoid the high-nitrogen formulas. Pest or disease control may be needed from time to time. When it is called for, take plants outside for spraying.

ROSES IN CONTAINERS

Even though roses growing in 5-gallon cans or the equivalent are a common sight in nurseries, surprisingly few gardeners think of roses as plants for container culture. Yet roses in containers are a possibility in any part of the country. Where winters are severe, winter protection is simplified since plants can be moved without disturbing the roots to a sheltered porch, garage, or basement—wherever temperatures can stay in the 15° to 25°F/−9° to −4°C range.

Before you decide that you're going to smother your patio or terrace with tubbed roses, realize that any container-grown plant is going to require more care than the same plant in the ground. Not that the care will be different; you just have to pay closer attention to the routine culture essentials. Watering, in particular, assumes increased importance. Because containers are exposed to the elements on all sides and have no direct contact with the soil, they dry out more rapidly than the ground does and have no subsurface water reserves to draw upon, beyond what is in the potting soil.

On the positive side, in some instances care of tubbed roses can be easier than care of rose garden plants, and often it will be better care because you can be more thorough. In watering, you'll know all roots have received their share when you see water draining out of the container. Spraying is easier and potentially more thorough because you can get at all sides of the tubbed plant. And fertilizer (especially liquid) goes on quickly and is directed entirely to the plant's root zone.

What roses to plant

As a general rule, the floribundas, polyanthas, and miniatures are best adapted to container culture. They tend to be compact, bushy, and of moderate height; and their habit is to flower almost continuously throughout the rose season. As a dividend, their cluster-flowering gives you a greater amount of bloom per flowering shoot than you will get from the larger but single-flowered hybrid teas. Virtually all grandifloras and the hybrid teas that have large or bulky bushes will be less satisfactory. If you want to try some hybrid teas in containers, stick to the shorter or thin-caned sorts.

Containers, soils, and care

Square or rectangular, straight-sided wooden boxes are the best containers for roses because they offer more root room than pots or round, tapered tubs. These are sold at most nurseries and garden supply shops, or by mail order, in a variety of kinds and sizes. If you're a handy carpenter you easily can make your own. Be sure planters are made from decay-resistant wood: redwood, cedar, or cypress. Don't skimp on the size of the container. A 14-inch-square wooden box is about the smallest you'll want to use for polyanthas and smaller floribundas, while hybrid teas and the more robust floribundas will be better off in 16 to 20-inch boxes. For any container, about a 16-inch depth is minimum. Filled with damp soil, any of these containers will be quite heavy. If you plan to move them from place to place, you might want to attach casters to the container bottoms or put each container on a platform with casters. If you choose the latter, make sure the platform has drainage holes that line up with those in the container.

Roses perform best when their roots are kept cool (one reason for mulching), but this is more difficult to control in containers than in the ground. Large wooden containers, frequent watering, and placement where containers (but not plants) are shaded will help. Another way to moderate container soil temperature—especially effective with miniatures—is to nest the container inside a larger one, then fill the space between the two with vermiculite. Space between the two containers should be one inch or more. Keep the vermiculite moist and it will act as insulation to hold soil temperature down.

Of greatest importance in a container soil mixture is the soil's structure: this is what determines the air-water relationship discussed on page 62. Your tubbed roses will need a well-drained and noncompacting medium. This is most easily achieved by mixing your garden soil with organic materials, such as peat moss or any of the commercially packaged planting mixes. If your topsoil is on the heavy (clay) side, use a mixture of half garden soil to half organic material; for lighter soils, you can use a greater percentage of soil—about two parts to one of organic. And for each container, mix in about a 4-inch potful of bone meal.

After you cover the bottom of the container with prepared planting mixture, set the bare root plant inside. You may have to bend the roots slightly to fit into the container, but they shouldn't be so long that they have to coil around the bottom. If they are, cut off the part that coils. Center the plant, spread out the roots, and fill in around them with the prepared soil, firming it well with your fingers around the roots and under the crown. When you are finished planting, the bud union should be about 1 inch above the soil and the soil surface about 2 inches below the container's rim.

After firming the plant in, water it thoroughly so that water runs out the drainage holes, saturating all the soil in the container. If the soil settles too much, add more and water it in until it remains about 2 inches below the top of the container. If the rose bush has also settled, jiggle it from side to side while pulling upward on the shank between roots and bud union until it returns to its proper depth. Do this during the time that the planting soil is flooded so you won't tear or break roots.

After growth begins, water often enough to keep soil moist but not soggy; never let soil dry out to the point that the plant droops. In really hot weather, check your tubbed roses daily just to be safe. Always give them enough water so that it runs out the drainage holes.

Because frequent and thorough watering continually leaches soluble nutrients from container soil mixtures, you'll want to fertilize regularly during the growing season. Liquid fertilizers are simple to mix and apply, are available immediately to the roses, and are the safest to use in containers since you can regulate the concentration in each application, regardless of how much solution you apply. If you fertilize about every 2 weeks after growth begins you should have roses in lusty good health all season. Should you prefer to use a dry fertilizer, be sure you use one that is completely water soluble so that undissolved elements will not build up in the soil. Apply dry fertilizer evenly, scratching it lightly into the soil, then water thoroughly. Conservatively follow recommendations on how much to apply, and use the fertilizer no more often than specified. The slow-release fertilizers, mentioned on page 76, are widely used for container plants.

THREE PROPAGATION METHODS

Every winter and early spring, nurseries bulge with sturdy bare-root rose bushes, and mail-order nurseries are ready to deliver equally husky plants at the drop of a letter. Why then, you might ask, should you bother to propagate roses when good plants are so available?

Various practical considerations aside, the chief reason for wanting to propagate your own roses is the pleasure of it. Words can't quite capture the satisfaction provided by beautiful blooms on a rose bush that you nurtured from a scrap of wood. Of course, if you want more plants of a particular rose that no longer is sold, or of one you can't identify, then you'll have to grow your own—either from cuttings or by budding onto understock plants. If you have the creative urge (and are somewhat of a gambler at heart), try raising entirely new roses from seed.

New plants from cuttings

Propagation from cuttings is the simplest way to grow additional plants of a favorite rose. Most vigorous roses—shrub and climbing sorts, most old garden roses, polyanthas, floribundas, grandifloras, and many hybrid teas—will grow well on their own roots. In most cases, a cutting-grown rose won't make much of an impression in your garden until its third year, at which point it is the same age as the newly planted 2-year-old bare-root bush from a nursery.

You can start cuttings from dormant wood at pruning time or take softwood cuttings during the blooming season. For dormant cuttings, select wood that's pencil-thick in diameter and make each cutting about 8 inches long. Remove the lowest two eyes, dip the end to be rooted in a rooting hormone powder (sold at most nurseries), and insert the end 3–4 inches deep in a pot or in the ground. If you plant directly in the ground, make a trench in the soil, put ½-1 inch of coarse sand in the bottom, and fill in around the cutting with a half-and-half sand and soil mixture. Firm the soil and water the cutting. For starting in pots, a light, sandy potting soil is the best. Start cuttings in a spot which receives little or no direct sunlight.

During the flowering season, you can start softwood cuttings from stems that have just bloomed. Cut off the faded flower just above the first 5-leaflet leaf and make the second cut farther down the stem just below a leaf; you'll want at least four growth eyes on the cutting. Cut off all but the top two sets of leaves, dip the cutting in a rooting hormone, then pot it in a sandy potting soil as described for dormant cuttings. Finally, water the cuttings in, cover the pot with a plastic bag or invert a glass jar over the cuttings, and place the pot somewhere out of direct sunlight. In a month or two, when new growth appears, you can remove the bag or jar. If you enclosed the entire pot in a plastic bag, you shouldn't need to give the cuttings any additional water during their rooting period. But if a glass jar is covering them, check often to be sure the soil doesn't dry out.

New plants by budding

Virtually all rose bushes sold bare-root are budded plants. At the proper time of year, professional budders slice growth eyes or "buds" from stems of the roses they want to propagate. They insert these buds into incisions in the bark on well-rooted cuttings, called "understocks," of another rose known to give good root systems. There are several good reasons for propagating roses this way.

• To the commercial grower it means faster production of new varieties: a cutting long enough to be rooted will have at least four buds, but each of these buds inserted into understock could produce a separate plant.

• The commercial grower also needs plants which can be dug up easily without damage to roots and which have roots that will pack and ship easily. Most commercial understocks have relatively flexible and not-too-thick roots.

• Some roses, regardless of the quality of their own roots, are difficult to root and would always be in short supply if they had to be propagated from cuttings.

Commercial growers who ship nationally also look for understocks that will grow well under the greatest possible variety of growing conditions. As yet, no perfect understock has been developed that is suitable for all regions, but two of the most widely adaptable are *Rosa multiflora,* a species from Japan, and the semi-double, maroon-red climber 'Dr. Huey'. Multiflora is preferred for cold-winter areas; 'Dr. Huey', with a shorter dormancy requirement, is better for most of the Southwest and other mild-winter regions. Other mild-winter understocks are 'Odorata' (an old Chinese garden hybrid) and *Rosa fortuneana*—the latter good for the unusual conditions in Florida where roses never go dormant and many soils are fast draining and nematode infested.

Perhaps the simplest understock source is sucker growth from any of the roses in your garden. If one got

Step-by-step budding

BEGIN by making a 1-inch-long T-shaped cut in bark of understock, an inch or two above soil level.

FOR BUDWOOD, choose a stem that has just bloomed. Slice under bud to get 1-inch bark shield with bud in it.

PEEL BACK understock bark at T cut, insert bud shield. Bud should be at least ¼ inch below top of T.

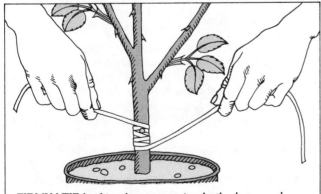

FIRMLY TIE bud in place, wrapping both above and below it but leaving bud exposed.

WHEN BUD sends out a strong new shoot next spring, cut off understock growth about 1 inch above it.

away from you during the previous year so that it grew long and matured its wood, you could cut it into 8-inch pieces and root them as described for hardwood cuttings on page 92. The only difference is that you'll want to gouge out all eyes on the cuttings except for the top two; any eyes left below the point where you would insert the bud are potential sucker sources.

Since your budding will be on a small scale and for your own amusement, all you need is something that roots easily and well and that will accept the majority of buds you put on it. Among the old rambler types, 'American Pillar', 'Crimson Rambler', 'Dorothy Perkins', and 'Veilchenblau' have been successful. If you live in a mild-winter area, you might also try *Rosa banksiae* and 'Climbing Cecile Brunner'.

Sometimes you can buy Multiflora plants for hedges or erosion-control plantings. These plants may be suitable for budding the summer after you plant them; just one, allowed to grow, will supply you with understock cuttings for years to come.

Whatever you select to be your understock, the process of budding onto it is much easier if the understock is grown in a container. Then you can perform the operation at table height instead of at ground level.

Spring and summer are budding seasons; the earlier the growing season begins, the sooner you can bud. The understock must be succulent enough so that its bark will peel back easily from the woody core of the stem.

You need two "tools" for budding: a very sharp knife and something to tie-in the bud when the operation is finished. You can buy special budding knives that assure you of a good, sharp edge. Some of these are made with flattened handles designed to lift the flaps of bark formed by the T cut (see drawing on page 93). Moistened raffia once was the standard tie for budding, but this has been replaced by rubber strips 5-8 inches long known as "budding rubber." Even simpler to use—because they require no tying—are plastic bud coverings. These are clear plastic patches which you wrap completely over the bud and clip together on the opposite side of the stem from the bud. Both plastic and rubber budding wraps are sold by horticultural supply houses. A good local nursery or your county agricultural office should be able to suggest a source for them.

Three to four weeks after budding, you should have evidence of your success or failure. Cut the wrapping and look at the bud you inserted: if it is plump and green, you have the beginnings of a new rose bush. If, instead, it is black and shriveled, don't despair; try another bud on the opposite side of the same understock and a little lower than the original.

New plants from seeds

Rose breeders wanting to produce totally new rose varieties pollinate one rose variety with another and grow hybrid plants from the resulting seeds. The activity is known as hybridizing and can be an engaging pastime for the home rose grower as well. The mechanics of hybridizing are so simple that insects, the wind, and the roses themselves do it with the greatest of ease and frequency. The hips that decorate many old roses in autumn or that you remove from your hybrid teas are the result of such natural forces at work.

At first you may want to plant seeds from hips that form naturally. Until the mid-19th century most new roses came from such unplanned crosses. Doing this will give you the experience of harvesting, planting, and raising new plants with the minimum of disappointment should any fatalities occur. The blooms on these seedlings are likely to spur you on to planning and making definite crosses—either because they are so fascinating or because they are so nondescript that you feel a little guidance is needed!

When to hybridize. In all regions where you can count on frosts in October, do all your hybridizing with the first crop of bloom in spring. Hips require about 4 months to form, mature, and ripen, and you want this process completed by the time cold weather arrives.

When mature hips turn orange, yellow, or brown, they are ready for picking. Usually this is in early autumn. In regions where the growing season is short some rose hybridizers cover the full-sized hips in midsummer with aluminum foil. This hastens ripening so that all hips will be ready by the end of the season.

An after-ripening period of low (but not freezing) temperatures combined with moisture is claimed by some hybridizers to improve the percentage of germination. As you pick the ripe hips, put them in boxes or plastic bags where you can cover them with damp sand, vermiculite, or peat moss. Then, put these in the vegetable crisper of your refrigerator. You can leave the after-ripening hips outdoors if you prefer, but see to it that they are safe from mice and squirrels.

Any time from the beginning of December to mid-January, remove the hips from their after-ripening quarters (they'll be black and partly decomposed by then) and shell out the seeds. These will be of odd sizes and shapes, but a convenient indicator of which are good and which aren't is the water test: plant those that sink in water; discard seeds that float.

Planting the seeds. Growers of rose seedlings have many favorite ways to plant and germinate the seeds, but they break down to two basic methods: either you plant the seeds close together in fairly shallow containers and transplant seedlings soon after they come up, or you sow them in flats or boxes where they will remain until they flower. The first method probably is more popular because, initially, it uses less space and less potting soil. But it does require more labor because you have to transplant. If you plant seeds where they are to bloom, use a flat or box at least 3 inches deep; sow the seeds an inch apart in rows about 2 inches apart. In either case, cover seeds with ⅜ to ½ inch of the potting soil.

Seeds often will start to germinate within 6 weeks of planting and will continue for about 2 months. The first two leaves to appear are oval shaped and not at all rose-like; it is the second set that proves they are roses. As soon as this second set is out, you can transplant the seedlings. As an improvised trowel to lift the tiny plants, use something like a nail file, knife, or ice cream stick; try to keep some soil around the seedling roots during the operation. If it is a cross you particularly value, you may want to keep the seed bed intact for another year. Some seeds which fail to germinate the first spring may grow the next year.

Growing the seedlings. Here again—as with seed planting—you have a choice of two basic ways to handle the seedlings: indoors or out. Traditionally, rose seedlings would unfurl their first blooms in greenhouses, but this was done mostly to beat the often miserable spring weather in England and parts of France where so much hybridizing was (and still is) going on. A greenhouse still is quite satisfactory but by no means necessary. You can just as easily flower seedlings indoors in a sunny window or under artificial light.

Any of these indoor methods are most popular with hybridizers living where long and cold winters make the growing season short. A bush hybrid tea seedling may bloom as early as 6 weeks from germination (climbers and old rose seedlings may take 2–3 years), so cold-climate gardeners can flower rose seedlings during winter and early spring before roses outside even have new growth. This gives seedlings the advantage of a long growing season the first year. During this period, the hybridizer has a chance to evaluate new plants early, then again on second and even third bloomings, before the season is over. As soon as spring frost danger is past, you can move your seedlings outside. Protect them from wind and direct sunlight for about a week, until they adjust to the outdoor atmosphere. If you wish to try them under artificial lights, use the 40-watt fluorescent tubes made especially for growing indoor plants. A two-tube fixture is satisfactory, a four-tube one even more so because of its better light distribution. Locate the lights about 6 inches above the containers in which the seedlings are growing, and leave the lights on for 16 hours each day.

Where winters are relatively mild, there's not as much to be gained by flowering the seedlings indoors. If you wish, you can prepare your seed beds outside. Just a raised bed with light, fast-draining soil could do for both germination and first flowering; although to save space you might want to germinate in flats or pots and transplant to the raised beds.

Damping off—a fungus which rots young seedlings at soil level—can plague seedlings of almost any plant. This is the reason for using sterilized soil and clean containers. As an added precaution, you may want to dust the seeds with captan before planting. Should any seedlings damp off, water the seed flats or pots with a fungicide solution or dust with captan. Mildew may bother seedlings, especially those grown outdoors.

Any seedlings you select may make fairly thrifty plants by their second or third year in your garden. But the only way you will be able to compare them fairly with commercially produced roses is to bud your seedlings onto one of the standard commercial understocks (see page 93). Sometimes you will notice improved blooms on your budded plants and you may get a larger, more vigorous bush.

How to hybridize a rose

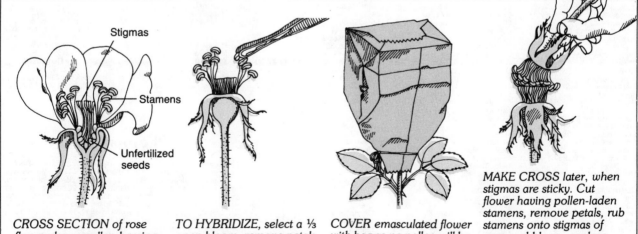

CROSS SECTION of rose flower shows pollen-bearing male stamens, female stigmas, and unfertilized seeds.

TO HYBRIDIZE, select a ⅓ open bloom, remove petals, and pull off stamens to prevent self-pollination.

COVER emasculated flower with bag so no pollen will be carried to it by insects or wind.

MAKE CROSS later, when stigmas are sticky. Cut flower having pollen-laden stamens, remove petals, rub stamens onto stigmas of prepared bloom, replace bag for week. If successful, ovary will swell.

Index—General Subject Matter

Index—Rose Varieties

Boldface numerals refer to color photographs.

Photographers

All-America Rose Selections Incorporated: 36 top left. **Derek Fell:** 29 top right. **Gerald R. Fredrick:** 30 bottom left, 44 top right. **Russell Lamb:** 1, 45 bottom left. **John C. MacGregor IV:** 8, 9 bottom left and top, 12, 13 bottom right and top, 16 bottom left and right, 20 bottom left, 22 top left and center right, 53 bottom right, 55 top left and bottom right. **Steve W. Marley:** 4 and 5, 19, 22 bottom left, 30 center and bottom right, 58 bottom left. **Ells Marugg:** front cover, 9 bottom right, 13 bottom left, 16 top left and right and center left, 20 bottom right, 21, 22 top right and bottom center, 28 top left and right and bottom left, 29 top left and bottom, 30 top left and right, 35, 36 top right and bottom and right, 37 top right and bottom left and right, 38, 43 top right and bottom left and right, 44 top left and bottom left and right, 45 top left and right and bottom right, 46, 50, 52 top right and bottom left, 53 top left and center and bottom left, 55 top right and bottom right, 58 top left and right and bottom right, 60, 61. **Jack McDowell:** 28 bottom right, 37 top left, 43 top left, 52 top left and bottom right. **Dick Reeves:** 20 top left. **Darrow Watt:** 22 bottom right, 27.